Radical Restoration

The Dawn Knighton Story
What can one face to face encounter with God do in your life?

DAWN KNIGHTON

ISBN: 1522967494
ISBN-13: 978-1522967491

FOREWORD

Dawn's story proves that nothing is impossible for God and that He can transform even the most hellish life and turn it around for His glory. She is a woman of courage, dignity and tenacity. The enemy tried very hard to steal her life, but instead she is being used by God to set women free from the darkest horrors imaginable. Never give up hope that with God you will win the battle.

Heidi G. Baker, PhD

Co-Founder and Director of Iris Global

DAWN KNIGHTON

ENDORSEMENT

This is one of the most amazing stories of redemption I have ever read and even though Dawn has shared many of her experiences with me, I couldn't put the book down once I started reading. I appreciate the fact that Dawn did not water down her story but shared it all in a way that can build your faith and change your life no matter what your personal circumstances may be.

I am always a person who examines fruit. I don't care what people say; I watch what they do and then try to discern the motivation behind it. The one thing I have seen in Dr. Dawn Knighton's life is that the power of God not only transformed her life, it is contagious in the lives her ministry touches. Reproduction tells me it's the real thing. There is fruit that remains. I have been able to visit prisons with Dr. Dawn and observe her ministering to groups and individuals and watch the tangible power of God work through her and I have watched her disciple women and see their lives blossom.

The main thing I want every reader to know is that Dawn is real, her experiences are real and the ladies who share their own testimonies in Chapter 19 are real. I have not only read *Radical Restoration, The Dawn Knighton Story,* I know the living epistle very well. I am the lady on the corner with the bullhorn and you'll just have to read the book to understand.

Dr. Kathy Tolleson
Kingdom Life Now Ministries

Dawn's story is so compelling and almost impossible to comprehend. It shows the redemptive power of Jesus Christ in its purest and simplest form. She has taken what most would call life's toughest challenges and come out on the other side a victor. And not only a victor but a shining example of our redeemer as she reaches back into to the prison system she escaped from and pulls men and women out to freedom in Christ. This is only the beginning of her story!

Love you to pieces!!
Pastor Sheryl Brady

I will never forget the divine moment in which I met Dr. Dawn Knighton in passing as I eavesdropped on her telling her story to someone else. Her story is riveting, dynamic, life changing, to say the least. Anyone who hears her story, cannot help but want to know her God. As she says it, she's "his favorite". Her story of God's saving Grace is unlike any other I have ever heard. Her book is definitely one of those you will not be able to put down, but even more, whether you have a relationship with her God or not, you will want one by the end of her book!

All My Best,
Tina Naidoo, MSSW, LCSW

CONTENTS

INTRODUCTION

It was late October 2003 and Daytona Beach was hosting another Biketoberfest, where bikers from all over the world come to ride and party. As the sounds of motorcycles roared in the background, I watched as the handle of a pistol came down toward my face. In mid swing, all I could see was a giant forearm with veins popping out and a big 8-ball tattoo in the center of it. He began busting me across my forehead over and over again. I remember asking God, "Is this it? Is this the beating that's gonna finally take me out? Am I really going to die this time?"

This was not an unusual scene in my life. A life of working for escort companies and dancing in strip clubs was a normal way of living. Here I was again in bed with a man I never met before just to earn enough money for my next "hit". I had been beaten up before. But this time, I knew something was different. My hands were taped behind my back and there was another strip of duct tape across my face. I was not able to speak or move. As I listened to the daunting words of my rapist, I felt totally helpless. He was telling me of the brutal, graphic, and inhumane things that he had done to other women while he was beating me to a bloody pulp. He went on about how he had killed them and how they deserved it. "You bunch of trashy tramps. You're nothing but no good crack whores. Y'all are all the same and you all deserve to die." As I squinted through the blood puddles that were filling my eyes, I could see that he looked like Satan himself. His eyes were black, his face contorted and sweat was pouring off of him like water. My face was throbbing, my ribs were crushed, and some of my teeth were missing as they had been knocked out. As he straddled me I winced, scared of the next blow.

I was crying out to God, "Please don't let me die like this." It was at that moment I felt an overwhelming sense of peace come over me. As I watched his every move, his countenance began to change. He started to gag and then began throwing up all over me. I couldn't believe it. I saw tears begin to roll down his face. He was actually crying. He sobbed and pleaded as he began to put on his clothes. He kept saying over and over, "I'm sorry . . . I'm sorry . . . I am so sorry for what I have done. Please just let me get out of here." With a huge sigh of relief, I thought to myself, "It's over! Thank You God! Once again, you have spared my life."

CHAPTER 1
THE VOID

As far back as I can remember I have always wanted to fit into the crowd. As much as I tried, I never felt like I could actually blend in. I always felt different and unwanted. Because I felt like an outcast, I would make up elaborate stories with imaginary people to try to make people accept me or to help me feel important. I would say or do anything that I thought would make people laugh, even at the expense of humiliating myself. It didn't matter whether it was true or not.

I would give away everything I had to try and get people to like me. I would even take my Mom's jewelry to school and give it to my friends thinking that just maybe that would make them feel special. Often times I would get in trouble because my new clothes would go missing. Before you knew it, my parents would see one of the less fortunate kids in my neighborhood wearing it proudly. I enjoyed the satisfaction of meeting a need and helping someone feel good and look beautiful.

I would honestly say that I have always loved God. I went to a Christian school through the third grade. Every Sunday morning I would get myself up and get ready for church. Then I would stand in my driveway and wait for the Sunday school bus to come and pick me up to go to the Baptist Church. I absolutely loved church, and I was there every time the doors opened. My Daddy often tells the story of how I would go and get saved and baptized over and over. My name was in every church bulletin in town. I would always go to the altar and ask for prayer. That always led to the church people coming to our home to talk to my parents about salvation, which they never appreciated.

I always looked forward to summertime because I knew my Aunt Mable and Uncle Bobby would come get me for a week or two to spend time with my cousins. They lived way out in the country on a beautiful piece of property with lots of land and giant oak trees. It had a beautiful sink hole full of fish that we fed in the evenings. We would ride motorcycles and bicycles, play on the trampoline, go fishing, and get very dirty. In the evenings, we would sit in a circle in their living room and read the Bible and talk about the stories we read. The best part of those summertime visits was that we would always go to church. They attended a little Assembly of God Church and my Aunt Mable's Dad, "Granddaddy Cooksey," (as he was called by my cousins and me) was the preacher. He would teach us the Word of God and he would be so passionate about what he was preaching that he would turn beat red and shout, "Glory be to God!"

It wasn't like the church I was used to at home, because he was on fire and every part of me would feel like I was about to burst with excitement and anticipation. I listened intently to every word he was saying. I wanted what he had; he had power in him like I had never seen before. The congregation would pray and touch heaven. I felt like angels were there with us and I felt the presence of God like I had never experienced. I loved it! I remember singing those songs out of those hymn books and they would make me cry. I loved the promises of going to Heaven, with streets of gold, and knowing Jesus was building me a mansion in the sky. I just couldn't get enough.

I was a child full of energy, very athletic, and always on the go. I loved to skate, and for many years I was on the speed skating team. And when I wasn't skating I was on the softball field every chance I could get. I was always roaming from house to house, going from this friend to that friend's house. I guess you could say I've got fire in my feet.

CHAPTER 2
FIRST LOVE

I will never forget the date of May 8, 1980. It was the day I met the love of my life. I had just turned fourteen years old. We went to the same middle school but I had never really talked to him. I was staying over at a friend's house and we went to a party. I still remember what I was wearing - pink overalls, a white tee-shirt, and pink high top converse tennis shoes. I felt so cute. I remember the first time I saw him. He had the most beautiful silky shiny blonde hair, freckles across his pug nose, and the sweetest smile that I had ever seen. As he came over and began to speak to me, he melted my heart. That was it; I was head over heels in love. Deon became my very best friend. He loved me like no one else and we became inseparable. We would talk for hours on the phone every night, after being together all day. His brother would come and pick me up, and we would all go to the movies. I will never forget one of our first dates together. We went to see the cartoon movie The *Fox and The Hound*.

As our relationship grew and we got older, we started getting into trouble. We would skip school together, which later turned into drinking, smoking pot, and taking speed. This progressed into weekends on acid, as well as Quaaludes, and then snorting cocaine. It didn't take long before we figured out it was easier and cheaper to sell drugs and make money, to get high for free. We were now our own best customers. By seventeen, I was married and pregnant with my first child. When she came into the world, she was the most beautiful little girl. She was a chunky little blonde-haired, green-eyed angel, and we were so excited. Unfortunately, as time went on our relationship unraveled and total dysfunction set in. Staying out late after work, going to the bars, and selling drugs drove us apart. We ended up divorcing, but we never fell out of love. We were soul mates. Approximately a year later, he was killed in a car accident and I was devastated.

CHAPTER 3
THE SEARCH

After Deon's death, my life began to really spin out of control, with many late nights. My life consisted of days with no sleep, and a drug dealing boyfriend, who soon became my second husband. It was a Friday night, February 27, 1987, at 7:00 p.m., and we were sleeping on our L-shaped sectional couch. We were getting some rest because we knew it was going to be a busy night. At this point in the game, we were dealing kilos, and had a lot of customers. All of a sudden, we woke up to a loud bang as the door was kicked in, and men in black with bright yellow letters on their backs that said F.D.L.E., began screaming at the top of their lungs. Pistols were pointed in our faces as they surrounded us. We were busted. I was about five months pregnant and on probation already. All I could think of was the nightmare of possibly having my baby in prison. They handcuffed us as they ripped our house to pieces. Their unmarked cars littered the street, and they hid behind the back of the house, awaiting the customers who would be coming to purchase their goods for the night. As each of them arrived, they were detained by law enforcement. By the end of the evening, there were about thirty people in the middle of our living room floor in handcuffs. They had to let some of them go, but the ones who had dope on them went to jail with us. We were shown on the 11 o'clock news, walking out of our front door in handcuffs, and next to our picture in the paper the next day the headlines read in bold print, *Ring Leaders: Community Drug Bust.* The reality of possibly going to Federal prison got our attention. We bonded out with a new outlook on life, and no more drug traffic at our house. Our home became as quiet as a deserted city. Only by the grace of God and a praying mother- in-law, our charges were dropped from a technicality on their search warrant. God was on our side once again.

That, my friends, was a wake-up call. We managed to stay somewhat clean and sober as I finished out my pregnancy resulting in a beautiful baby boy. He was the most handsome man in the world, and he still is in my eyes. Fourteen months later, along came another little blonde-haired, green-eyed angel. Life was good. We were working hard and spending most of our weekends at a rental house on the beach. We were cooking out at the home, and having a social drink and maybe a joint or two.

Once Again

As my children got older, ballgames and cheerleading began, and we were always at the ball field. I began to meet new people and make new friends. Before I knew it, I was headed down the wrong road again. I was snorting cocaine with one of the other moms from the baseball team. She would come over to hang out, and always had a pocket full of coke. Once again I was staying up all night, losing weight, and drinking like a fish. It wasn't long until I was completely out of control. Good old addiction was taking over my life again. I was writing bad checks, got a DUI, and had multiple car accidents and incarcerations. Once again, I was going through a divorce and had no stability.

It became a pattern. I would get into a relationship, get married, get back on drugs, and go back to jail, over and over again. This time, I decided that I would put myself into a rehab program. I did the best I knew how to try to change. I got a head full of clichés and tools that were supposed to help me to stay clean and sober; Eventually, I mended my relationships with family and my children AGAIN. I got a great job cutting hair and making great money - AGAIN. Needless to say, once AGAIN it didn't last long. Two weeks before I graduated from a one year long program, I got mad and walked out. At point, I was never able to finish anything and would constantly sabotage myself. Within fifteen minutes of leaving the program, I had $500 worth of crack in my hands and I was off to the races.

CHAPTER 4
SLAVE TO SIN

One day, I decided I would use one of the tools I had learned in rehab. I would try a geographical change. My boyfriend, who happened to be my ex-husband, wanted to learn how to work on boats, so I found a school in Daytona Beach for him to go to, and we were off. I had it all worked out, as I could actually accomplish a lot when I was clean. We got him in school, found a nice apartment, and put all three kids in school. I landed a great job cutting hair at a barbershop. The only problem was that I didn't make enough money to support all five of us. So, I decided to get a second job at a country and western bar in town, and it doesn't take a rocket scientist to guess what happened next. Once AGAIN, I was off to the races!

One shot, (of meth, barbiturates, or heroin - whatever I could get my hands on) led to another, and then I was doing lines of cocaine, and taking diet pills to keep me awake the next day so I could cut hair. Then, I would be back to work at the bar until three in the morning. I was spiraling out of control AGAIN. I knew then that I was not headed in a very good direction. I didn't want to hurt my kids anymore, so I thought that it would be best for them to stay with their grandparents until I could get myself back together.

Needless to say, I did not get myself back together and things went from bad to worse. I was running around with "sugar daddies." I was a beer tub girl during Bike Week, and not long after, was dancing in the strip clubs and working for escort companies. I would make thousands of dollars, but it was spent as soon as I got it. The more money I made, the more drugs it took to keep me numb. Money, materialism, men, and drugs had taken me over. I married men who were paying my bills, and manipulated every person I came in contact with because I valued no one, especially myself. If my lips were moving, I was lying.

Dead on My Feet

I had come to a point in my life where I could not even stand to go fifteen minutes without smoking a hit of crack or doing a shot of meth. I would have to shoot a pill (of opiates) and have a drink to come down so I could work. By this time, I was in a constant daze and I couldn't even remember my children's birthdays or even remember Christmas and other holidays. I couldn't stand to even live in my own skin. My parents didn't know if I was dead or alive. I couldn't allow myself to become sober enough to think or feel. While working in the strip clubs during Biketoberfest, I went from club to club, dancing, robbing men, and selling drugs. As my drug addiction was getting worse, so was the quality of the men. I was beginning to go downhill fast. I never dreamt this could ever happen to me. How did I get like this? It took all I had to actually eat and to maintain a little meat on my body; I looked terrible, like someone off of a horror show. I remember one night staring at myself in the mirror and actually seeing the devil in my own face. I was staying up for weeks at a time, seeing demons and shadow people everywhere; I was walking around in a state of paranoia everywhere I went. I trusted no one, not even myself. One trick after the other, life had become a nightmare. Tricks were getting crazier and crazier. Abuse became the norm. I felt dead on my feet.

And then came the night I thought my life was coming to an end at the hands attached to the 8-ball tattoo. As I woke up in the hospital's rape crisis center, I remember the nurse telling me, "You are not alone; everything's going to be o.k." I laughed inside; I had never felt more alone in my life. I have to say that I was completely hopeless. There was such a big part of me that just wished that he would have killed me. I felt like the dirtiest and trashiest person on the face of the Earth. Every part of my being had been violated. I had bald spots all over my head. My hair was missing from where it had been pulled out in chunks, my teeth were missing, and my nose was broken and packed with gauze. I had stitches in my crotch and could hardly move because so many of my ribs were broken. As I lay in that hospital bed I asked myself, "Now what?" All hope was gone.

CHAPTER 5
DEATHS DOOR

It wasn't long at all before I was out of the hospital and at it again. I had to stay high and I was on a mission AGAIN, knocking at death's door. I hooked up with the dope boys and went to work. A Glock, (9mm gun) and a pocket full of drugs was all I needed. I would take men to motels and put the gun to their heads, and rob them for every last penny they had. I would blind fold them, tie them to a chair, and promise them a lap dance. The next thing they knew, I had stolen their car, wallet, phone, and used all of their credit cards.

Things began to get really ugly. My addiction was worse than ever. I was drawing the water for my shots out of puddles on the asphalt, and using used cotton out of an already smoked cigarette. My shots were getting bigger and bigger. I was having seizures in hotel rooms and waking up in puddles of vomit. I was doing a suicide triathlon; smoking crack, shooting meth, and then doing a pill to bring me down. I was living from trap house to trap house, getting robbed, shot at, stabbed, raped, used, and abused. Spending hours on the street corner was my life.

I remember the corner on Belleview and Ridgewood that was a block from the trap house where I stayed. There was a beautiful, old mansion on that corner. It was amazing, and had gold lions in front of it with a gorgeous manicured yard and beautiful flowers. There was this lady that lived there, and she would come running out of her door with a bullhorn every time she would see me yelling, "This is a no prostitute zone. Remove yourself from the area. The police will be called!" She even put "NO PROSTITUTION ZONE" posters up on the telephone poles and trees. The posters depicted a woman with her hand on her hip in a provocative pose, but with a circle and a big **X** over it. Needless to say, we were not very fond of each other at that time. One night, I remember getting in a car and being dropped off hours later at my corner, all beat up and bloody. That same lady's daughter saw me and brought me water and washed my face and prayed for me.

I had absolutely no desire to live anymore. In my eyes, I was a complete failure. I was in and out of jail on a regular basis. I would get arrested, raise all kinds of hell in jail, and get tied down in the black chair. Sometimes the guards would have to use the taser to get me to confinement. Everyone at the jail knew me on a first name basis. I was a regular, and they hated to see me coming. I remember a sweet lady by the name of Ms. Anne that came to teach a Bible study. They were having a service and I went up for prayer and told them, "I can say this salvation prayer, but I don't know how to be a church lady. I don't know how to be like you." So she came and picked me up upon my release and took me home with her. It lasted about two weeks and then I decided to call one of my old guy friends to meet me at the movies. When we got in the theatre, he began to fondle me. It made me mad and I walked out and started walking back to Ms. Anne's house. A couple in a car stopped to ask me directions and I asked them for a ride. Sure enough they were smoking crack. The devil always has the wrong people in the right place. Needless to say, it was on after that. I was supposed to get baptized the next day, but I just couldn't make it. I was too ashamed and couldn't stand the fact that I had disappointed Ms. Anne. It sealed it – I just knew I couldn't be a "church lady."

Stuck in the Pits of Hell on Earth

Every time I went back, it got worse. I couldn't see light in any area of my life. I was completely hopeless. I would find myself sitting in old abandoned crack houses with no running water or electricity. Roaches and rats were the only thing moving. Once, I had even sat in a trap house where the dog had starved to death and laid there, dead for days. I was so tormented because I knew there was no way out. I would sit there for days because I was so paranoid. I could literally see demons and shadow people all around me. I would go behind the restaurants at night and eat out of the dumpsters, scared to death a rat was going to jump out at me. I would go to the Boardwalk and climb under the steps of the pier and sleep where I felt I was safe. I will never forget standing at the dumpster at the Krispy Kreme waiting for the day old doughnuts to be dumped into the trash. I couldn't stand living in my own skin. I hated myself. I had burned absolutely every bridge and had hurt every person that had ever loved me or tried to help me.

CHAPTER 6
HE HEARD MY CRY

Day after day, and night after night, of living and working the streets left me desperate. There were many nights that I cried out to God for help. I said, "God if you are real and you love me just give me a sign." I can't even begin to tell you of how many days that He fed me and how many nights that He kept me safe. He was always sending special people in my path. On the way home from one of the many times that I tried to get clean and sober and go to church, God brought to my attention a house on Ridgewood Ave. by the name of *Heaven's Gardens*. I felt like the Lord was telling me to contact them, so I called. A lady by the name of Pastor Aida invited me to visit. It was a house for prostitutes and women just like me. Because I was trying to stay clean and sober at the time, I wanted to volunteer and give back, so I would go and cut and color the ladies hair, buy groceries, and help any way that I could. I thought what she did was the most amazing thing I had ever seen. She loved me when I felt unlovable.

Pastor Aida encouraged me and showed me the love of God. She even took me to a Charisma Fire Conference in Orlando. At the conference I thought, "These people are crazy!" They were running around screaming "FIRE" and speaking in tongues. I thought the streets were crazy until I went there. I remember sitting in the conference and a lady who had been delivered from prostitution was speaking on what God had done in her life, and it began to give me hope. She came down off of the platform and prayed for me. It was like she could read my mind. As she prayed for me, I felt like she knew everything I had ever been through. The conference was truly amazing and something that I will never forget. I wasn't sure what everything was about, but I was sure they had the power of God in there. However, it wasn't long until I was back out on the streets. I was so sick and tired of being sick and tired, in and out of jail, and in and out of sobriety. I was always just trying to survive. Every time I would just start to get back on my feet, I would fall into deeper sin and hopelessness; but I cried out to God and He heard my cry.

Sitting in an abandoned house in the wee hours of the morning smoking crack and shooting meth, I began to feel the presence of the Lord. After being up for days, I felt the urge to go to church. I went back to a church that Pastor Aida had taken me to, Calvary Christian Center, in Ormond Beach. They had a homeless ministry there so I went, got showered, got clean clothes, had breakfast, and sat through a Bible study. Then we went into the sanctuary. I had to go into the bathroom and use drugs just to stay awake in the service. You see, it had been days since I had slept. Pastor Jim Raley preached an amazing message that gave me a blessed assurance that God really heard my cry. Strung out as all get out, I ran to that altar as fast as I could and I cried out to God to save my soul and do whatever it would take for me to change. Pastor Dawn Raley came and laid hands on me and told me that Jesus loved me and that I was royalty, and a child of the Most High. I felt amazing, but that feeling was short lived because when service was over, I was back to the streets. But I knew that I had experienced a true encounter with God.

Apprehended

It was only a matter of a couple of weeks after that service that I was arrested and charged with my last five felonies. I was in a raggedy old car, with a stolen tag, no driver's license, and a half ounce of crack. As I turned the corner on 13th street, I saw the lights come on. I was busted! I began to throw crack out the window to get rid of the evidence and ate the remainder of what had fallen in my lap. The cops came running to the car screaming, "Get out of the car with your hands up!" I was hand cuffed and put inside the cop car as they searched my vehicle. They found the crack cocaine that I had hidden in my floor board, and I was incarcerated once again. I will never forget the ride. I had eaten enough crack to kill a cow. As I sat in the back of the cop car, I was higher than I'd ever been. I remember the words of the police officer telling me, "You can do better than this. Give your life to Jesus and turn your life around before it's too late." I thought, "Is he seriously talking to me about God right now?"

As usual I went in with a fight; kicking, screaming, and cussing, which led me to straight confinement. Locked down in an 8x10 cell and restricted in a turtle suit (straight jacket), buck-naked and freezing cold, I cried out to Jesus once again, "God, is there any way that you can help me?" I was in the jail inside of the jail, which was the maximum security confinement of the entire compound. It had now become a matter of life and death to me. I had said the salvation prayer forward and backward, upside-down, and sideways. I needed the real deal; I needed an absolute mind and heart transformation that would penetrate the depths of my soul.

It was at this time that God began to truly speak to me. He began to give me a vision and speak to me, telling me that I was valuable to Him, that I was a precious jewel. He shared that He had put me in His safety deposit box and reminded me that I cried out at the altar that day for Him to do whatever it was going to take. He took me to a place of total surrender. He showed me that He was with me in my broken place. He was going to heal my hurts and my wounds, and take away the shame and the pain.

I was taken out of the turtle suit and placed in a room by myself. It was then that I asked Officer White to bring me a Bible. She and I had a love-hate relationship. I would come in a mess and she would have to fight me, and then she would encourage me once I came back to my right mind. As I read it, I began to receive revelation, and was reminded of the promises of God that I knew as a little girl. I remembered memorizing John 3:16, "For God so loved the world that he gave His only begotten son, that whosoever believes in Him shall not perish but have ever lasting life." WOW, I was amazed at this promise. It gave me so much hope. I spent hours reading and reading.

DAWN KNIGHTON

CHAPTER 7
BLOOD TRANSFUSION

I knew that God was giving me another opportunity at life, but I knew I had a lot of work to do. You see, I had always loved God, but I didn't know how to be like Him. I never thought I pleased Him or thought I was good enough. My shame was always a wall of separation. I thought He was mad at me when I made a mistake, and I had made a bunch of them. I was full of hate, bitterness, and resentment. I hated everybody, but most of all, I hated myself. I was my own worst enemy. As I sat in that cell, I was overcome by the presence of God. I asked God to manifest Himself to me so that I would never be the same. I cried out and said, "God if you are really real and You love me and if you will deliver me from all of this bondage and set me free, I will spend the rest of my life telling people what you have done."

The more time I spent on my face crying and seeking the presence of God, the more I was able to picture Jesus. It took my relationship with Him to a whole new level. I would picture myself in His lap, crying on His shoulder. He would stand up and hold me like a little girl and dance with me. Pretty soon, I could see myself snuggled up to Him when I went to sleep and I would lay my head on His chest and hear His heart beat. Our relationship grew closer and closer.

Falling In Love with My Savior

He showed me visions of a prison that I had inside myself. I knew that the Word told me that I had to forgive in order to be forgiven. He took me through the process of healing from every person that I held captive inside of me. Every day we would open another prison door. Jesus and I would walk hand in hand and pray.

I would forgive them, I would forgive God, and I would ask God to forgive me for my unforgiveness. Then we would walk each person out and I would pray that He would never allow me to hold anyone in prison inside of me again. The hardest of all was forgiving me. I would have flashbacks of the people I had hurt, the abandonment and neglect of my children, and I would think about how selfish and self-centered I was before. I would have flashbacks of the people I had robbed and hurt. The Lord began to speak to me through the words, "I shed my precious blood so that you would be forgiven, so who are you not to forgive yourself?"

It was at that moment that I gave it all to Him. It was truly a blood transfusion. He told me that if I was the only person on this Earth, He would have still gone to Calvary just for me. HE LOVES ME! I gave Him all of me and I asked for all of Him. I cried out to God for Him to give me everything it was going to take for me to truly surrender. I felt hot from my head to my toes, like hot oil was being poured all over me. It was at that moment I began to speak in tongues. It was the most precious time of my life. I could feel the presence of God so thick, and it was tangible. I could touch Him. The hardness, the bitterness, the anger, the resentment, and the unforgiveness all began to melt, and the love of Jesus flooded my soul. As I prayed, I could feel His healing virtue. Just like the Bible says. . . I would sense rivers of living water. I was falling in love with my Savior.

I remember the Lord speaking to me so clearly one day as I was reading in Isaiah. It was Isaiah Chapter 61. It said, "THE GOOD NEWS OF SALVATION, 'The spirit of the Lord is upon ME, because the Lord has ANNOINTED ME to preach good tidings to the poor; He has sent ME to heal the brokenhearted, To proclaim liberty to the captives, and the opening of the prison to those who are bound; To proclaim the acceptable year of the Lord, and the day of vengeance of our God; To console those who mourn in Zion, To give them beauty for ashes, the oil of joy for mourning, the garment of praise for the spirit of heaviness; that they may be called trees of righteousness, The planting of the Lord that he may be glorified.'"

I began to ask the Lord, "What could you possibly anoint me for? What could you ever use me to do?" The Lord began to show me myself, and all the other women that I had come in and out of jail with, over and over again. We would get arrested and go to jail, say a prayer, read our Word, and go to church, just to get released to go back to the same street. If we went to prison, we were released with $50 and a bus ride back to our past. The Lord began to give me such a clear, strong vision of having a house for women like myself. I just laughed at the very thought of it. I said, "I can't even take care of myself, much less other people like me, we are a real mess! Where would I even start?" I had no idea how it would happen, but what I knew for sure was that it was a vision from God.

Soon after, I was released into the general population section of the jail, and then came the day to go before the judge for my trial. I was facing a 15 year prison term, but by the grace of God, was sentenced to six months of Jail Addiction Treatment Program (J.A.T.P.) and after that, only a year and a day in prison. Once again, I experienced the tremendous hand and mercy of God.

One of the ways that the Lord would reveal Himself to me was through the church services we had while I was in the J.A.T.P. They made such a difference in my life. I will never forget one night soon after getting out of confinement. There was a lady by the name of Ms. Carolyn that came in to do service with us. One of the first things she said was, "I have a Word from the Lord for someone here, it's out of Luke 4:18." As I looked up the scripture and read those words, I said, "OH MY GOODNESS; IT'S FOR ME!" It was out of Isaiah Chapter 61. That was the first time that I had a real confirmation from God. I had been crying out for Him to make Himself real to me and He did.

I shared my vision with Ms. Carolyn and we prayed. You could feel the Spirit of God all over during our prayer. Also during my time in J.A.T.P., one of the inmates who was leaving gave me an MP3 radio player. I skipped recreation so that I could listen to Pastor Raley at 1pm every day as he preached his sermons on the radio. God had given me a spiritual father to speak into my life to teach me about Him. It seemed like every sermon fed me to the max. I would laugh and then I would cry. I would take notes and teach the other girls in my dorm about what I had learned. I even had the opportunity of leading one of the officers in the salvation prayer.

DAWN KNIGHTON

CHAPTER 8
TRANSFORMATION

It was a set-up from God himself! It was transformation time. As I would lie in my bed and look at the ceiling, it looked like a cocoon. I guess it was some kind of fiberglass, but the Lord told me, "You came in as an ugly little worm, but you will leave here my beautiful butterfly." I would get in to my Bible for hours just tearing that Word up. I was so hungry for more.

One of the ladies that came to teach Bible Study at the jail, Ms. Cynthia, would send me books that her father had written on deliverance. Me and my 'bunky' would stay up late and read by the light in the crack in the door. We would say all of those prayers over ourselves and pray the demons out of each other. She became my best friend and would read to me for hours. Our cell was like a miniature church or prayer closet; people would come in for prayer and counseling. Life was going so good. Then, before you know it, we got called out for the "prison run." This was the unannounced time that we were sent to prison to serve out our sentencing. We had prayed and asked God to send us together. He answered our prayers and away we went. I knew that it would be a couple of weeks before I was able to talk to my mom on the phone again. She was such a great encouragement to me even though she was terrified by the thought of me being in prison. She had always been my biggest cheerleader. It seemed like forever before I received my pin number and was able to call her again. I was so thankful for the restoration that God was doing in our relationship.

Receiving and Orientation in prison was quite interesting. Any modesty that you may have had left was ripped from you as soon as you got there. Stripped down naked, standing in the hallway with a line of other woman, we were sprayed and given shampoo for lice, and a good ice cold shower. Then they teach you how to bend over, squat, and give a big cough, so they can look up your butt to make sure you are not smuggling anything into the prison. Imagine the humiliation. I then got in line with wet, "deloused", tangled hair to get my D.O.C. picture taken for my badge that I would be wearing on the front of my shirt for all to see.

Fighting for Freedom

Even though I had been in the presence of God and going through some deliverance, I was still struggling with some attitude issues. I went through *Receiving and Orientation* and then it was off to T-Dorm (confinement dorm). I had the pleasure of spending some time with the most precious lady by the name of Marie. I grew to really love her. She was a little bitty thing, but very feisty. She ran the place. She had been in prison since 1968. We would stay up until wee hours of the morning and she would teach me about Jesus. I absolutely loved listening to her tell me about her relationship with Him. She took me to our little window and showed me how the razor wire was shaped like a heart. She told me that was her promise from God. She was doing a life sentence, but had the promise of eternity in her heart.

I have to say, going to prison was the best thing that could have ever happened to me. One of my favorite parts of my journey was our Chapel on the Annex. I had to fight to get to go because only a certain amount of people could go from each dorm, but I was always at that door or the first one in line to sign up on the Chapel list.

I will never forget the first chapel service I attended. Our Chaplain came out and greeted us and you could tell by the way she carried herself that she was not playing any games with the devil. She was a very nice lady and carried herself as a true woman of excellence. She came in with a beautiful dress and gorgeous shoes to match, and a hat that topped off her outfit. She came in and started us off in prayer and then led us into worship. As we sang, the spirit of the Lord would fall in that place and the whole chapel full of women were dancing, praising, shouting, and singing. I could feel the chains falling off of me as we danced and worshipped. It was amazing.

It wasn't long until "Chap" put me in the choir and I was loving life. I loved her Sunday services. Her messages were always right on time. They were always the Word from God that I needed. Then we always had an amazing deliverance and healing service. We would be in church most of the day and I loved every second of it. Chap would lay hands on me and I would go out in the Spirit and come back, only to go back up for prayer again. I remember telling my friends, "If you ever see me fall out, you better know it's God." Then BOOM, I was out. This thing was real. I was so bound by demons that when Chap would pray for me, I would vomit and snot would sling until we finally got all those devils out. One time in the Chapel, I remember singing, and the Lord spoke to me and told me to run. I ran back and forth across the front of the chapel. As I was running and sweating, water was pouring out of my hands. The Lord showed me I had healing fire in my hands and fire in my feet. I was running out my redemption.

I needed more; I was on fire! I was so hungry for the Word, and the chapel assistants helped me to sign up for Bible college so I could further my education. I knew that I had to do whatever it took to retrain my brain to a new way of thinking and that it would be done by the transforming Word of God. All I wanted was to be totally set free.

Joy Unspeakable

A few days later, as I was standing in the pill line waiting to get my psychotropic medications, it felt like my tongue was stuck to the roof of my mouth. The Lord spoke to me and told me to go and pray for a lady that was sitting on a bench by the building. I had never seen this lady before in my life, so I stood there and argued with him because first of all, I didn't know how to pray out loud, and second of all I didn't want that lady to think I was nuts. I had been diagnosed by the doctors as being bipolar and schizophrenic and had taken so much Seroquel and other medications. Well, I stood there and fought with Him, but it wouldn't go away. Finally, I said, "Okay, fine." I wasn't scared to approach people for the wrong reasons so why should I be scared to do this. I went over and asked her if I could pray for her and she began to cry. She showed me her nail beds. They were all purple and she told me she had just had heart surgery and didn't know if she could make it back to her dorm. I prayed with her and walked her back to her dorm. That day the Lord said, "You are healed." I have never taken another one of those medications again!

For the first time in my life, I had joy unspeakable. I couldn't even explain to people what I felt on the inside. It was indescribable joy and peace. This was freedom I had never known before. I was happier than I had ever been and I was still in prison! My chains were gone, and it felt euphoric. The birds were more beautiful than ever; the grass and trees were greener than I had ever noticed them being. I felt like my eyes were opened for the first time ever. I was forty years old and felt like I was living for the first time. I had never seen a person that had been delivered from a twenty-six year addiction to crack. But I told God, "If you will get me through this and deliver me for good, I will come back to this prison and tell everybody just how real You are. I promise You that."

CHAPTER 9
THE PLANTING OF THE LORD

After a few months, I was called to pack up for a transfer from the prison to another unknown location. I was devastated. I had gotten so close to my bunky, Marie, and I spent all my free time with my best friend, Amie. Above all, there was no way that God would allow me to leave the Annex Chapel. It had become my safe place. But, yes, it was true - I was being transferred. As I packed my belongings and walked out the door, Ms. Marie told me, "You continue seeking the Lord and walking in His Presence and you are gonna be unstoppable. Don't you worry about me and don't you ever look back."

I will never forget that day. It was about 3:00 a.m. on a rainy morning. I got wet trying to get to the gate with all of my belongings in my pillow case. I felt as if it was the end of the world. I couldn't imagine what God was thinking. Then I climbed up in this old raggedy white bus that had metal across the windows so you couldn't see in or out. As we started down the road, I could hear the water sloshing back and forth in the toilet bowl. It was accompanied by the most horrific smell I had ever experienced. It was definitely a ride I will never forget. I was absolutely traumatized; I thought, "This is it. What in the world could possibly be next?"

As the bus pulled into this little bitty camp in the middle of nowhere land, I asked myself, "What in the world am I supposed to learn in this?" As we got off of the bus I asked the correctional officer where we were and she said, "Levy Forestry Camp, in Bronson Florida." It was so hot. It was a very small compound and only housed about 300-350 inmates. I remember that day like it was yesterday as I felt so discouraged. I was assigned to C dorm and sent on my merry way. As I walked toward the building with the big C painted on it, everyone stared as I came through the door of the old block building. As I went over to the officer's station, I couldn't hear a thing she was saying because of the roaring of the giant window fans. They roared like jet engines. I was assigned to a corner bed. I was C-1 6 upper, which meant I was in a corner top bunk. I was glad to see I had a window by my head and my feet. I didn't know what to think, and I was suffering from severe culture shock. As I began to get settled in I moseyed outside and started to recognize a couple of people that I had met on the bus. We hung out since we were the new girls on the compound. I looked around on the property as one of the girls showed us around; she took us on a tour. The first thing I wanted to see was the church. OH MY, was I surprised! It was a small room with some chairs and a podium. But it didn't really matter to me, because I knew that Jesus was in me and that everything was going to be okay.

As the days went on I came to really love Levy. I would take my Bible and go out and sit on the basketball courts and read the Word. The Lord would always meet me there, and as I read, He would speak to me so clearly. I remember sitting out there while the doves would come and eat in the grass where I was sitting. I could feel His presence all around me. God was giving me revelation like never before. I just had such a hunger for more of Him; I wanted to go deeper and have more understanding of His Word. I would sit out there day after day, searching the Scriptures. After a couple of weeks or so, I was assigned a job at St. Andrews Nursery working on a tree farm. I would get up at 4:30 every morning and go into our T.V area so I could see. I would do my morning devotions with Jesus before getting ready to go out to work. I would read whatever Chapter in Proverbs that corresponded to that day in the month. I had learned that there are 31 Chapters in Proverbs - one for every day of the month. I also knew it was the book of wisdom and God knew that I needed plenty of that. I also did a prayer every morning that I had found in a book. The prayer was called *The Commanders Prayer*. I got it out of a book that was given to me. It was written by the same lady that had prayed for me and read my mail at the Fire conference that I had attended in Orlando with the ladies from Calvary Church.

My first day of work was very intimidating. I had to be dressed, shirt tucked in, belt on, and nothing in my pockets. We would stand in line at the gate house to be searched before we went out to work. I would stand there as the sun was rising and just stand in awe of the Glory of God, just so thankful to be alive. He gave me peace even though I was scared to death. The next thing you know, out of the gate I went. We got on a big white bus and it was off to the tree farm. I was so blessed and excited to be riding on a bus looking at the fields and all of the cows. I had never thought cows were beautiful until then. We arrived at the farm and went inside of this giant warehouse looking building. There was a giant tree planting machine. Over the next few months, I had the opportunity of working at every part of the process of planting and growing trees. It was such a blessing. The Lord also taught me about the principles of discipleship during this time.

I started out working on the soil tilling machine. I would empty big bags of soil into this giant bin. It had a big wheel that would break up the soil. Then it was put into little potting trays. The next part of the process I worked on was where the seeds were dropped into the little pots in the trays. I had to make sure it was only one seed per pot, and that they all got a seed. I stayed there for a few weeks. I was moved to the fertilizer machine where the trays were run through and fertilizer was sprinkled in each little pot. I had to make sure that we kept the fertilizer bin full at all times, because without fertilizer the seeds wouldn't make it. And from there it went through the watering process and then we stacked the trays on a trailer. A tractor would pull us out in the field where we placed the trays out for the trees to grow. Then we would bring them in to take the weeds out, and put them back out to grow. Next, we would pull them, wrap them, and then load them on a semi to be shipped out to the world. I loved working out in the field. I loved the hard work. It was so satisfying to feel like I was accomplishing something. The whole process was Jesus teaching me all about discipleship.

I remember being out in the field one day with some of the girls. We were working when one of them asked me to pray for her because she was about to reach her EOS (end of sentence) soon.

We stopped what we were doing and I prayed for her with all of my heart. I was on a thirty day fast and had been asking God to show me my purpose and to manifest Himself to me. And boy, He did that day! As soon as we finished praying, I looked up at the sky and there was a rainbow in the cloud. I was so excited because I knew it was for me. I couldn't wait to get back to that dorm and get in my Word and find out just what that meant.

God's Assignment for My Life

When we arrived back at the compound I went straight to my bed to read my Bible. I looked in the concordance and it was in Ezekiel 1:28. "Like the appearance of a rainbow in a cloud on a rainy day, so is the appearance of the brightness all around it. This was the appearance of the likeness of the glory of the Lord." Then I read, Ezekiel 2: 1-8 "So when I saw it, I fell on my face and heard a voice of one speaking. And He said to me, Son of Man stand on your feet and I will speak to you. Then the Spirit entered me when he spoke to me and set me on my feet and I heard Him who spoke to me and He said to me, Son Of Man, I am sending you to the children of Israel to a rebellious nation that has rebelled against me, they and their fathers has transgressed against me to this very day. For they are impudent and stubborn children. I am sending you to them and you should say to them. Thus says the Lord God, as for them, whether they hear or whether they refuse-for they are a rebellious house. Yet they will know that a prophet has been among them. And you son of man do not be afraid of them nor be afraid of their words. Thou briers and thorns are with you, and you dwell among scorpions, do not be afraid of their words or dismayed by their looks. Thou they are a rebellious house. You shall speak my words to them whether they hear whether they refuse, for they are rebellious. But you son of man, hear what I say to you, do not be rebellious like the rebellious house, open your mouth and eat what I give you."

And that was it. The assignment had been given. I now had purpose for my life. I knew that God was going to send me back to the streets and into the prisons to teach and preach His Word. I knew that all the hell that I had come through would not be in vain. I knew that God was going to teach me to teach and counsel others that had been in the same lifestyle. I also knew that God had given me a vision to have houses. There was nothing worse than watching my sisters come into prison, surrender their lives to Christ, and ninety days before leaving begin to cry because they had no place to go. There was nowhere safe to continue what the Lord had started in their lives. I knew that in order to be able to carry out an assignment like this for God, I needed an education. I did every Bible study that I could get my hands on; I was in every church service that we had. I knew I had to be washed by the water of the Word of God and would spend my weekends studying and memorizing scriptures.

My bed became a counseling center. Woman after woman would come to me for prayer and a scripture; they would come and ask me for a Word to encourage them for whatever battle they may have been facing at the time. I would pray for them and fast with them to see the needs and issues they struggled with be met. We would sit in awe of the supernatural things that God would do through our families. It was amazing watching the restoration that was taking place.

Dawn's Mugshot

Dawn after Prison Fight

Radical Restoration Beach Baptism

Dawn with Tina Naidoo with Texas Offender Re-entry Initiative

Dawn with the Mayor of Daytona Beach, Derrick Henry

Changed Lives

My Hair Salon for the Elderly

CHAPTER 10
END OF SENTENCE

Even though I was incarcerated in the middle of nowhere and most people would have thought it was a terrible thing, I was going to miss Levy. I had developed amazing relationships with the officers and staff. They made such an amazing impact on my life. On October 7, 2007, this part of my testimony was complete. It was the end of my sentence and I have to admit it was a bittersweet end. The ladies had become real sisters to me. Going back through that gate was a very scary thought, but I knew that I could do All things through Christ who strengthens me, (Philippians 4:13). I will never forget "master count" on my last night there, and saying my DC number for the last time. I knew that God promised that one day my DC number would turn into a pin number that would give me prison access. I knew if I continued to walk in radical obedience to the Word of God and to be faithful in what He told me to do I would walk in every promise that He had given me.

The day had finally arrived. I couldn't sleep at all that night, so excited, but emotionally terrified to walk out of that gate. As I waited in the yard watching to see my dad's car drive up, I was thrilled to wear my new EOS outfit - a real pair of jeans, a bright colored top, and leopard flip flops. As I paced anxiously waiting for my name to be called, it finally came over the loudspeaker. I picked up my giant brown box full of books that I had accumulated over my time and ran to the gate house with such anticipation to see my family. The EOS process seemed like it took forever, but in reality it was only a few minutes. As a lieutenant walked me to my father's car, everything on the inside of me was screaming, "Jesus, I pray that you will keep me and do a work in me so that I can come back and show my sisters just how real You are!"

As we approached the car, my dad and stepmom came out to greet me. Oh what a joy it was to see my family again! As we pulled out of the parking lot I looked back to see all my sisters that I left behind standing on the yard waving good bye. I will never forget thinking just how blessed I was to have a family to go home to because so many of them did not. I knew in my heart that God had called me to be the one to help fix this issue. My heart's desire was that there would not be one woman or man that had begun to change their life in prison without a place to continue to be discipled. On the ride home, my dad stopped in Crystal River at a restaurant. I got the biggest seafood platter I could find. It was delicious; I think I even ate the parsley. What a great feeling it was to be free, not just on the outside but on the inside too!

I was so excited! I had not seen my mother in years. Pulling into her driveway, I had butterflies. But there was also so much joy because I was home. I walked in my mother's house to see my family for the first time in a long time. I hugged my mom, my step father, and my two youngest children. But to my surprise, there sat an old acquaintance of my past, right in my mother's living room. He was all dressed up in black, cell phone on each side and a blue tooth on his ear. I had noticed a brand new shiny car in the driveway on the way in but did not realize whose it was. It was the head of the Cuban Mafia from Miami. My mom thought he was the sweetest man but they had no idea who was sitting in their living room. The devil pulled out the wealthiest, most powerful person from my past that he could find. There he was, the devil himself, sitting in my mother's living room, attempting to give me a brand new car and money. He even had given my mother money to buy brand new clothing. I told my mom to take a picture of us together because I knew it was a memory that I would never forget. He ate dinner with us and then I thanked him for coming and told him that I had given my life to Jesus completely. Then I said, "I rebuke you Satan In the Name of Jesus Christ, you can get in your brand new car, take all your promises, your money, and your drugs, and go back to the pits of hell where you came from."

CHAPTER 11
THE PROCESS

For the first few weeks, I stayed close to my mom and we had a great time of restoration together. God restored our relationship and brought us to a place where we were close once again. The Lord had given me a vision in prison to remodel my mother's bathroom, so I did. That was my first project when I came home. We did it together and I have to say it came out beautiful. After about six weeks, I began looking for a job in the shopping center close to my mother's home. There was an Indian eyebrow salon with a "Stylist Wanted" poster in the window. I went in and applied and got the job. I was very insecure about going back to work. I had not cut hair in some time and I had missing teeth and a resume of approximately forty-six felonies. The enemy tried to convince me that nobody would ever hire me.

But they did, and for days and days I sat and looked out the window praying for customers. It was an eyebrow salon that had not had a stylist in a long time so it wasn't very busy, but it gave me time to get into my Word and to ease back in society. The people I worked for were from Pakistan. They would come into work and light their incense, go in and worship their god while I prayed and worshipped mine. I prayed for them, and they prayed for me. I knew that God had me there for a reason. The lady I worked for would tell me almost every day how God was pleased with me and I would tell her that Jesus loves me. Many days I would leave my Bible or whatever Christian book I was reading on my hair cutting station to see the next morning that someone had been reading it. I knew it had been moved. Although the lady I worked for was Muslim and I was a Christian, we loved each other very much.

One day when I was sitting outside the salon praying for customers to come in and watching the people walk by, I saw my old friend, Howard. He told me he worked at the barber shop four doors down and asked me if I wanted a job. I was elated. I walked over and they hired me on the spot. So I went back to work that evening and told my Indian friends that I was moving over to the barbershop and I worked both places until they closed and moved away. I loved working at the barbershop, but I thought to myself, "Lord you really like jokes. I've come from a life of prostitution and now I'm surrounded by men in a men's barbershop."

The Joy of Giving

I loved my new job, and it was conveniently within walking distance from my mother's house. On my walk to work I would listen to my MP3 player and praise and worship all the way there. I worked with three wonderful Christian men, Mr. Mack, Howard, and Ben. They were like family to me. Mr. Mack was older and tender hearted like my grandpa. Howard and Ben watched over me like big brothers. In the beginning, my work was a little slow and I enjoyed the fellowship. One of my biggest struggles after coming out of prison was finding a church to attend. I went to several different churches before I found one that really understood my zeal and excitement from being delivered from a twenty-six year addiction to crack cocaine. I found a church up on a big hill close to my mother's house. I loved it there. The pastor had just started a drug rehab for men in Tallahassee; he was the perfect pastor for me. As I got to church one Wednesday night and walked across the church yard, I noticed that the grass was very high. I thought to myself, "This grass really needs to be cut." I heard a voice on the inside say, "You cut the grass." I kind of chuckled to myself as I went in the door and enjoyed the Wednesday night service.

Later that night, while lying in my bed, the Lord continued to speak to me about cutting that grass. I couldn't imagine what he was trying to tell me. The next morning as I woke it was still on my heart. As I went through my day of cutting hair I had a customer hand me a business card from a men's ministry lawn care service. I laughed and knew it was straight from Jesus. So I called my pastor and asked him if I could cut the grass and he said, "Yes, what a blessing that would be because the lawn mower is broken." I called the men's ministry and asked them to go out and give me an estimate to cut the lawn at the church. It was approximately four or five acres, overgrown and neglected, something I knew I couldn't tackle myself. The guys called me at the barber shop and gave me an estimate of $300. I knew that with all my heart that this was something I had to do and at the time I had $319 in my checking account. I told the guys to go ahead and do the job and to give me a call when they were finished so I could come up and pay them. Later that afternoon they called and said that it was finished. I called my mom and asked her to come pick me up and to bring my checkbook. She drove me to the church to pay the guys. She was having a fit because I was giving that money away. She did not understand because I was supposed to be saving my money for my teeth, but I did it anyway. I wrote the check for $300, trusting, believing, and obedient to do all that God told me to do. The next day I went to work and was busier than I had ever been. And from that day forward, I don't think I ever made less than $300 a day.

As time went on, I continued to send stamps and money back to my friends that I left behind in prison. I tithed to my church faithfully, and blessed every homeless person I could find. I knew that God had blessed me to be a blessing to others. I wrote out my short term goals and long term goals. Within the first three months of having the grass cut, I was financially able to get $8,000 worth of dental work. I paid off all my tickets and fines and started working on getting my license back. It cost me $6,900 dollars to clean up most of the wreckage of my past.

Every day when I walked to work I walked past the Nissan dealership and I would pray, "Lord, if one day you would give me a car, I would drive the wheels off of it helping other people like myself. I would take woman to church and teach them about Jesus." One day I was cutting hair and one of the guys came in with a red Nissan shirt on to get a haircut. I asked him what the cheapest used car was that he had on the lot. He told me to save up a down payment and come in and ask for him. I did just that. I saved up my down payment, I went in and little did I know, he was one of the owners of the lot. Jesus made a way for me to be able to purchase a brand new car. The only problem was I did not have my license back yet, so my mom came and drove the car to her house. I continued to walk to work and complete what I had to do to get my license back. Walking to work while knowing I had a brand new car in my driveway was a very humbling act of obedience. Finally the day came when I got my license back and was able to drive for Jesus.

CHAPTER 12
THE BIRTHING OF A MINISTRY

One of the first things I did was find a Bible college and Seminary to continue my education in the Word of God. I knew that I would have to know it in order to teach it, since I was still walking with the vision of having homes for women. I will never forget that day I walked in to sign up for school with my checkbook in my purse. I had saved enough money to begin my education. I went into register and the registrar was not in but the chancellor of the school met me at the door. He brought me into his office and I filled out all of my paperwork as he explained the school to me. As the time came for me to pay and I wrote out my check, I realized it was October 7, 2008. It was exactly my one year anniversary from being released from prison. I was overwhelmed and tears began to flow down my face. I was walking into another one of the promises that God had given me. I began to share with Dr. Morris the reason for my tears and shared my testimony. Right then and there he gave me a full scholarship to Covenant Bible College and Seminary. I was very overwhelmed at going back to school at forty-one years old. School had never been one of my favorite things to do. I quit at sixteen, got my GED and started cutting hair. I never thought I would ever go back. As I read through the paperwork of writing a term paper, I knew that I didn't even know where the power button was on a computer! I had absolutely no typing skills whatsoever. But I knew that the Word of God told me in Philippians 4:13, "I can do all things through Christ who strengthens me."

I continued working in the barbershop while going to school, and God began to open doors for me to begin to minster. I would cut hair for the girls at the children's home and share my testimony of how God brought me out of addiction. I volunteered to be a counselor at the woman's pregnancy center in my community and I also counseled women in a homeless transitional halfway house once a week. The Lord also really put it on my heart to go back to one of the rehabs I had been in, where my old counselor was now the director. I shared with her what God had done in my life and she had me start doing groups with the ladies there. Shortly after, I was taking them to church on a weekly basis. I would use my church's van and load up approximately fifteen to twenty women, and take them to church with me. I knew I had what they needed. It wasn't long after that my pastor asked me if I would be willing to lead a group for people who struggled with addiction and I said, "Absolutely!" He told me to come up with a name. I began to fast and pray, seeking the face of the Lord on what he wanted me to call the ministry. He began to speak to me about the birthing process and then the care needed for a child's development. A baby needs to be held gently and often, fed, and nurtured. Through this process, the baby grows and matures. He told me this process was one of "Radical Restoration." I realized that this would be the name of my ministry. It would be a ministry of discipleship, growth, development, and ultimately, transformation. So, I started hosting small group meetings on Friday nights with about four women. I was faithful and I poured my life into these young women. I taught them everything I knew and was constantly seeking the Lord to teach me more, so that I could, in turn, continue to teach them. As the months went on, we would have up to three hundred in attendance. There were times where we would have more attendance on Friday nights than in the Sunday service. God was doing amazing things in my life. He was using me to teach others a new way of life.

He is Faithful

It was approximately nine months after my release from prison, and I had shared my vision of a home for women with a countless number of people in my community. God would have to perform a miracle, though, as I didn't have nearly enough funds for a project like that. I was doing outreach one day and a lady I had never met before asked to speak with me. She told me that she had vision of me in her house and God spoke to her about renting it to me. She described her house in detail, and as soon as the outreach was over I went down and took a look at it. The property was thirty miles from nowhere, in a small fishing village in Panacea, Florida. There wasn't a whole lot going on there, but rather it seemed like a community that needed love. As I walked on the property, I saw that it was an old cracker house; the front door was falling off the hinges. Walking through the house, I noticed boxes everywhere as it had been a gift shop at one point. There were rats and roaches because nobody had lived there in quite some time. I prayed as I walked through the place and asked God, "If this be your will Lord, then you make it happen." I left that day very encouraged, but also knowing that I had my work cut out for me. But I knew in my heart I was willing to do whatever Jesus asked me to do. I knew that on my own, I couldn't do it, but I also knew the promise that nothing was impossible with God. The next day as I cut hair in the barbershop, a friend came in for a haircut. As he left, he handed me a cashiers check, and told me that the Lord told him to give it to me. Little did he know, it was the exact amount I needed to put down on my new house in Panacea!

A couple of days later I went to visit a small little country church with about fifteen members. The pastor asked me to stand up and give my testimony. Afterward, they took up a love offering and it was the amount I needed to turn on my electricity. He did it that fast! Within three days, I had the finances I needed to start my first ministry house. I began calling paint companies, asking if they would donate paint. My family helped me clean up the yard, the house, and helped with repairs, so we could get the house up and running. In the meantime, I picked up a second job. Not only was I working in the barbershop, but I was also running my own hair salon in an assisted living facility. On November 7, 2009, we had our open house. It was such a great feeling knowing that now everyone could see that my vision had finally come to pass. The God I served was real!

I started out with four women in this home. We would all get up at 5 a.m. and do our morning devotions. I would drop them off at work and go work my two jobs. In the afternoons, I would pick them up, and we would always find a church service to attend. Again, I poured my heart and soul into these women. I taught them basic skills that we take for granted, such as having good hygiene, having manners, opening a bank account, balancing a checkbook, and being responsible at a job. More importantly, I was hungering for more of the Lord and was teaching them that as well. We laughed and cried together; we worshipped and we served. The Lord helped me devise a whole structured program covering health and hygiene, training to succeed in the world, spiritual warfare, and intimacy. Out of those first four women, the first graduate of my program assisted me in opening up two more homes for women in Tallahassee, FL. Since 2012, she has lived there and works as the director, overseeing the activities of the homes. The second graduate relapsed unfortunately, and ended up dying of a drug overdose. The third one is now a teacher outside of Atlanta, Georgia. The fourth one is happily married, and it was my pleasure to perform the wedding ceremony, as it was my first that I officiated. She now has one child and is enjoying her family.

After my first year of ministry, I felt the Lord leading me to open a thrift store. We had an overabundance of clothing donations that came in for the ladies and no place to put them. I felt that it would be a great way to help carry the financial responsibilities of our home. I looked and looked all over town, but every place was so expensive. I had prayed about what we could afford and the Lord put on my heart not to pay over $350 a month. One morning I was walking around my yard and the Lord brought to my attention the old abandoned house right next door. It faced the highway and was on commercial property. It was right outside my backdoor, so I called around and found out who owned it. He rented it to me for the price I needed and within forty-eight hours, we had it cleaned, painted, and up and running for business. Our first day of business was the day of the Mullet Festival, so there was a lot of extra people in town. Even with every piece of clothing priced at $1, we made enough money to pay three month's rent and utilities! The thrift store became such an incredible blessing to the people of our community and it opened the door for me to help more women. It helped teach the women in the ministry job skills, and gave them the responsibility of going to work every day. The more we blessed others, the more God blessed our store.

As time went on, I would see so many people in our community that were less fortunate. The Lord laid it on my heart to begin a food pantry and clothing closet. Every other weekend, we would have a line of people standing outside our door coming to get food and clothing. The Lord had blessed us in abundance. Never in my wildest dreams did I ever think that God could use me, not only to help these women, but to be a blessing to my community as well. He had brought me from homelessness to feeding the homeless. The Lord began opening doors that I had never dreamed possible.

Late one night, the Lord put it on my heart to write my chaplain a thank you letter and to tell her of all of the amazing things that He had done in my life since I had been released. Well, I did just that. I got up and began to type her a long letter letting her know of the goodness of God and of all the miracles that He was performing in my life. I shared how He was bringing to pass the vision that He had given me while I was in prison. She wrote me back and told me how proud she was of what the Lord was doing in my life and through my ministry. The letter was published in the *Compass Newsletter,* which was sent to every chaplain who worked for the Department of Corrections in Florida. Little did I know, one of my customers at the barbershop where I had been working at, was the head Chaplain for D.O.C for the entire State of Florida. He had observed me since I had come out of prison since he had been coming in every few weeks for a haircut. Without me knowing it, he watched as I opened our ministry and was walking out my God-given destiny.

By this time, I was three years out of prison and teaching at the Wakulla County Jail. I was in my third year of Bible College and I had started a mission satellite school for Covenant Bible College and Seminary as part of my own ministry. Again, the Lord's grace visited me, and each one of my students became eligible for a five year scholarship so she could earn her degree and further her education in the Word of God.

I loved teaching in the jail and ministering to the woman who struggled with addiction in my community. I would share with them everything that I learned, but my heart was still yearning to minister in the prison. At my three year mark, I called the chaplain and expressed my desire to get into the prison system. I applied for a pin number, which would allow me access, but I was not approved. He told me to call back in six months. I was devastated; I wanted so badly to go back. Six months to the day, I called him back and applied again. This time, God had answered my prayers and I was going back into the prison! The same head chaplain that had watched me transition back to society and start my ministry, called me and gave me the news. It was a Holy Ghost set up! Only God can do stuff like that. There was no way I should have been allowed to walk back through those gates, considering all of my felonies and wretched behavior from the past - BUT GOD...!

On Mother's Day of 2010, I was asked to speak for the Mother's Day program at a Women's Correctional Facility in Quincy, Florida. It was a day I would never forget. As I went in with my ID, I was searched and given a PBA (personal body alarm). Shaking like never before, gates buzzing and clanking as I stepped back into my rebellious nation, I was led into the auditorium where they were putting on the Mother's Day Event. Another of God's promises was coming to pass.

I remember vividly that I was sitting in the chair waiting to deliver my message as the keynote speaker. All of a sudden, correctional officers ran at me and surrounded me from all sides. I freaked out because I didn't know what was happening. It was my first day to minister at the jail and my emotions were already heightened. I didn't want to do anything wrong. As it turned out, I had accidentally pushed the button on my PBA, and the guards were all coming to help me. We all, especially me, had quite a laugh.

What a privilege and honor it was to have the opportunity to encourage my sisters and share with them the testimony of the restoration that God had done in my life. I had always asked God to let me be the one to come back and show just how real He is and He did just that. He allowed me the opportunity to come back as the one who had been delivered from a twenty-six year addiction to crack, men, a life of prostitution, and the love of money.

I was asked to return to the correctional facility on a weekly basis and teach discipleship in the life skills class. I was so excited about the opportunity, and I taught on living an uncompromised life of obedience to the Word of God. I have such a passion for helping others like myself to retrain our brains to a new way of thinking. I am committed to removing the false identities that the world and our past failures have given us and restoring the true identities that the Word of God has given us. I knew every Word of the Bible was true and I was passionate to share it with others.

DAWN KNIGHTON

CHAPTER 13
GETTING BACK UP

My last marriage was emotionally, physically, and spiritually abusive. It almost derailed my ministry – but God...

During my season in the streets in my addiction, I was very close to one of the men that fed me dope and sold me. My relationship with him was as sick as I was. I thought that this man loved and cared for me because he kept me high and in hotel rooms. He spent intimate times with me telling me how special I was to him. I was his bottom (his main B). I was no more special than the other poor addicted souls that were stuck in hotel rooms all over the beach making money for him. It didn't last too long until he was arrested and sent back to prison where unfortunately he had spent most of his life.

A couple of years after my release from prison, I woke up in the middle of the night with my old pimp heavy on my heart. I lay in bed and prayed for him and rebuked the devil at the same time, because I knew the man was no good for me. As I laid there, my curiosity could not stand it, so I got up and looked him up under the corrections website. Sure enough, he was back in prison. I prayed and decided I would write him a letter telling him all of the amazing things that Jesus had done in my life - how He had set me free and given me a vision in prison. And I wanted him to know it was all coming to pass. Not long after, I received a letter from him. He was so excited to hear from me and shared of his vision about a men's program. He wrote and told me how he had surrendered his life to Christ and gotten his Master's Degree in Religious Studies.

Changing the World

We just knew it had to be God setting us up to change the world for Him. We wrote and talked on the phone for the remaining time of his sentence. I will never forget his EOS (end of sentence) day. I was so excited; I had not seen him in eight years. I just knew that the Lord had saved us and set us free for a time such as this. I brought him home and had a full wardrobe of new clothes, shoes, and everything he could possibly ever need. I was so excited to see how the Lord was going to use us for the good. We were a Bonnie and Clyde for the bad and I knew we would really be a huge threat to the enemy together for the good. During his first week out, we did a march against addiction in downtown Tallahassee and then I praise danced and shared my testimony on the front steps of the State Capitol. It made the 6 o'clock news.

He had such an anointing to teach and preach. We would have Bible College on Friday nights and people from our community would come and do classes with us. Life was amazing, but that was short lived. It wasn't long before the sneaky behavior, lies, and deceit began to surface. I tried my best to hide the dysfunction in my marriage from the ministry, but it became obvious. I did my very best to be a Proverbs 31 woman. I wanted to be a good wife. I continued working in my two salons and going to school and began traveling to the prisons to preach and do outreach. Even though I knew things were not good in my marriage, I was determined to continue to stay on fire for Jesus.

Trouble in Paradise

While I was out of town, one of the ladies that had formerly been in our program and relapsed, was texting my husband. Apparently, they had been meeting while he was supposedly at work and had developed a relationship behind my back. One Monday while I was working in my Salon at the Assisted Living Facility, I received a call from Lisa, (the young woman who had relapsed) telling me that she had been at a motel room with my husband over the weekend and apologizing for what she had done. The first thing I asked her was, "Where are you?" It was obvious that she was very drunk, because she told me. Only by the GRACE

OF GOD did I not go and kill both of them in a rage. I began praying with everything that I had inside of me; it took all I had to finish the hair that I was doing and get out of there.

But I tell you, God is faithful. He began to remind me of my life scripture, Psalm 62:5, 6 *"My soul wait thou only upon God for my expectation is from Him. He only is my rock and my salvation, he is my defense, and I shall not be moved."* I knew I had a whole lot of people believing in me, including my family, my children, and people in my ministry. This was a tactic of the enemy, and I wasn't going to fall for it. I went home and confronted the issue and of course all I heard were lies. The text messages continued through the night and then she began drunk calling me and trying to torment me. She continued to tell me the things that they had done. I lost it! I was busting mirrors and felt the spirit of murder. All I knew was that I had to get away. I took a ride to the beach and prayed. Thank God, the Lord met me and spoke to me. He told me to take a couple of days away, to pray and to calm down, so I did.

His Love Tested

I ended up going to Daytona for a week and resting in HIS presence at a friend's house. It was so amazing. The Lord just poured his presence into my broken heart and helped me to come back around. I came home and forgave my husband and gave him yet another chance. The last thing I wanted was another divorce. I had already had seven divorces. I wanted this to work so badly. I just knew we were capable of doing big things together to advance the Kingdom. About eight months later, while we were on vacation for my birthday, I received a phone call from the girls in the ministry telling me that on their way home from Church they had found Lisa sitting on the side of the road, homeless and hungry. I have to admit, my first reaction was, "What do you want me to do about it?" He told me to take her in, feed her and take care of her. Here I was in the middle of a store arguing with God as He was KILLING MY FLESH. He told me to take in what I felt like was my worst enemy.

The girls stopped, fed her, and called me and asked if they could help her. After some squirming and fighting with the flesh, I told the girls to take her home to the ministry and to feed her, give her some clean clothes, and take care of her until I got home. It was a quiet ride home. I got in the car and told my husband about my phone call. He just looked at me like I was crazy. I knew I had to be obedient to what God was telling me to do.

My husband dropped me off at the ministry and I went in and gave Lisa a big hug and told her I loved her. I reassured her that everything was going to be alright and prayed with her. It felt so good to be able to do that. I had defeated the enemy. Lisa stayed with us for a few weeks as she began to get a little more stable. She decided that she wanted to go to the mental unit to try and get stabilized on her medication, so I took her. I asked the secretary to call me before she was released and I would come and get her. Well that never happened. While I was in Daytona doing an internship class for my doctorate, I got a phone call asking me if I knew Lisa because my name was on her emergency contact card, and I said, "Yes." She had been found unresponsive from an overdose and had been taken to I.C.U. I rushed home to see what I could do. I called her son who was taking his finals for college and tried to encourage him. It was all that I could do. I knew that she was not expected to live so I went to the hospital and prayed for her. Later that night, she passed away. Her kids did not know what to do nor did they have the means to bury her so I arranged and paid for it all. We had her body cremated and I had a nice funeral service for her. I gave her ashes to her son. The Lord reminded me through this whole ordeal that His Word tells me in John 15:12, *"This is my command that you Love others as I have loved you."*

Crying Out

I continued to be the best wife that I knew how to be, hanging on to every word of God's Word, fasting and praying for a breakthrough. I was crying out to God for direction in my marriage because it was getting worse each day. I never knew what or who I was going to come home to. He was being unfaithful to me, but I just continued to pray. I came home one day, though, and he lied to me right to my face, and I admit that something blew up inside of me. I hit him in the jaw with all of my strength; I just couldn't take it anymore. Crying out at the altar the next Sunday, I knew that I needed a miracle in my life. That day I had a special lady come over to pray for me. After praying, Dr. Margaret invited me to go to a conference for restoration. Heidi and Rolland Baker, Bill Johnson, and Randy Clark, were all ministering at this Voice of the Apostles conference. It was truly a time of healing for me. The Lord was using these mighty men and women of God to help restore my soul. However, at that conference, I received a call from my Dad. He told me that the doctors had found a cancerous tumor that had wrapped itself around his carotid artery. He was facing chemotherapy and radiation treatments. It felt like every man in my life was under heavy attack. I cried out to the Lord and He began to give me peace as He poured His love into me. As I received prayer I rolled around on the floor of that conference and was hurting more than I could ever remember. My Dad did go through chemo and radiation but I knew his true healing had come from the Lord that day. He is completely healed and knows that it was Jesus who healed him. My heart rejoices because now my Dad is saved. I met some special women there, including Ms. Mary Jo and her friends, Joy and Donna. They prayed for me and then Ms. Mary Jo asked me to come to her office at Charisma Publishing where she did some counseling and praying with me. It was so healing. I will never forget it. I left her office and as I was driving the Lord spoke to me; He said, "You always pray for others to be healed, why don't you pray for your loose tooth?" So I pulled off the interstate and God healed it, and even to this day, it's still hanging on.

The next week while I was cutting hair, my husband called me and said he was a suspect in a robbery. I knew right then my Father had heard my cries. My husband was arrested, and I knew in my heart that our marriage was really over. During this time, I was on my face crying out to God and standing on every promise of His Word. I had felt I had failed once again. I continued to pray for him, but he just could not stay out of jail. The Lord spoke to me that I could not fix him, try as I may. Everyone makes their own choices, whether it be for life or death, healing or destruction. Unfortunately, my husband continued to make the wrong choices and our marriage ended up in divorce. I continued to seek God with all my heart and I pray that one day, he will choose to do the same.

CHAPTER 14
FROM GLORY TO GLORY

As I continued going into the prison to share my testimony and spread the Word of God, I could see the need for a ministry house in Tallahassee; one that was on the bus line which would make it easier for my ladies to get jobs and go to school. As I was working away in my salon one day, one of my clients came in for a haircut. His name was Mr. John and he asked me how the ministry was coming along. I shared with him our need for another house. And sure enough that next Sunday he shared my vision with his Sunday school class and some of the men in there stood up and donated the money for the financing of our next house.

I was able to find a beautiful brick house with three big bedrooms and three bathrooms for only $35,000. Two of the bedrooms were large enough to fit three sets of bunk beds, so that I could provide a bed for a large number of ladies. I always pray for discernment about who to bring into my homes, but my heart has always been to receive anyone who truly wants help and not turn anyone away. The property also had a one-bedroom apartment in the back, like a mother-in-law suite. We loved it and worked very hard to make it a nice place to live. On November 7, 2011, we had our open house for this, our second home, in Tallahassee. We named this house after Mr. John and his wife, *The Coulter House.* They helped us not only purchase it, but to restore it and to furnish it. They are truly a blessing. God supernaturally used them to give us provision and funding. Once again we walked into a mess, but with prayer and a lot of elbow grease, we painted, scrubbed, cleaned, and got it all up to par. It was so beautiful to see many of my girls from the Panacea house come together to paint, scrub, clean, and restore this house in Tallahassee. They wanted their sisters who would be coming out of prison to have a place to live and turn their lives around. We opened up that house with a total of twelve beds and they were full before I knew it.

Today, this house in Tallahassee is run by my first graduate, Hollie. She lives there with her husband and their son. Hollie's testimony includes a life of dysfunctional relationships and drug addiction. Her son, Harrison was taken away from her when he was a small child. She came to my home in Panacea and the Lord utterly changed her life. She worked out her case plan while she was in our program and was awarded back custody when he was three years old. He is now nine, and has grown up in the ministry. He now has his own ministry in that neighborhood taking all of his friends to church. It's not unusual for Hollie to have fifteen kids loaded up in a van taking them all to church. He will be the first to tell you to this day that he is the Director of Radical Restoration Ministries, Tallahassee.

One day while riding down the road in the pouring down rain, I passed by a piece of property that had been for sale and abandoned for years. It was only a couple of blocks away from our thrift store and the first ministry house that we were renting. I had always liked the property; it was an old three bedroom house with a tin roof and a big front porch. It also had four small apartments on the property, like an old fish camp, but it had really been neglected. I had called on the price of the property several years earlier and it was quite expensive. It was priced somewhere around $200,000, but I noticed that the realtor sign had changed. As I was passing by it, all of a sudden the voice of the Lord told me to turn around and call about the property. As I continued to drive, He continued to unction me to turn around, so I did. It was pouring rain, but I turned around and got the number off of the new sign and called the realtor. I asked him how much they wanted for that property and he said that they were asking for $50,000. He said that the property was in probate and that the family just wanted to get rid of it. I told him that I would have to pray about it and then get back with him.

Here I was once again looking at property with no money and no credit. However, I knew that my Heavenly Father owns all the money and has perfect credit, and if He wants us to have something, He will make it happen. And He did. I felt the Lord leading me to offer them $25,000, so I called the man back and told him my offer. He was very angry. He told me that the price I gave was an insult, so I apologized to him and assured him that by no means did I ever intend to insult anyone. But, that was the price that I felt my Daddy had given me, so I hung up the phone and wrote the offer out on paper and sent it to them. They accepted it! HOORAY! But now he told me that I would have to come in and sign a contract on this property. That sounded great, but I had no idea where the money was going to come from at that moment to pay for it. I was scared to death, but one thing that the Word of God has taught me is to walk by faith and not by sight. So I did - I jumped out of the boat like Peter did in the Bible. My little disciples and friends thought I was crazy, but I did it anyway. When you know that you know that God is telling you to do something, it doesn't matter what people think. In John 2:5, Mary tells the disciples, "Whatever He tells you to do, DO IT." I knew I had to be obedient.

I started praying and fasting and begging God to show me how this was going to happen. I took my ladies over to the property and we anointed all four corners with oil and claimed and named the property for Jesus. We decreed and declared and everything else I could think of over the property, including all of God's promises. Then one night after church, I shared with my pastor what the Lord had done. A few days later he told me that the church was going to finance the property for us interest free. The property was in horrible shape. There was no wiring or plumbing and the floors in the house were falling apart. Nobody that I took there could see the potential in the place, but me. My ladies thought I was genuinely crazy.

I had so much excitement, and I just knew it was going to be awesome. We worked and worked our fingers to the bone. We replaced the plumbing, and my son helped us to rewire the electricity. We put in new flooring, and sanded, stained, and varnished the beautiful wood in the apartments. It was the most amazing transformation. We moved into that property and loved every second of it. It was so convenient. We could walk to the thrift store and the Dollar Store, which was right next door.

I continued working at my two hair salons, overseeing the ministry, and continuing my education. By this time, I had earned my Bachelor's degree and my Master's degree. The Lord had healed me of the learning disabilities and I was hungry to study His Word even more. I was traveling back and forth to Daytona for some counseling classes to finish up my doctorate. As I frequently returned to Calvary Christian Center, I would often join them in the homeless outreach, as well as Midnight Angels, going back into the strip clubs to minister with the Midnight Angels, a ministry to the dancers of the local strip clubs. On a monthly basis, groups of women would visit local clubs and take pizza and toiletries to the performing ladies, as well as encouraging words and prayer. I loved it.

Back to My Rebellious Nation

The Lord began to prompt me that I was going to be returning back to Volusia County. I tried my best to ignore it, but the passion for the lost and broken people in those streets and clubs just continued to get stronger and stronger. The Lord began to show me that it was part of the rebellious nation that God had given me as my mandate in prison. He spoke to me, that all of this time in Panacea and Tallahassee was training ground for where He was taking me. I was extremely comfortable in the very small town of Panacea, and Tallahassee had been my home town. I thought to myself, "Lord, you must be kidding!" Daytona was the last place on earth that I wanted to live. I loved coming for the weekends to visit, but I could never imagine coming back to live.

I was remembering the first time that I had returned to Daytona after getting out of prison. It was early in the year 2011. I had seen information online about a conference at Paula White's Church in Lakeland and Bishop T.D. Jakes was going to be there. I told my girls all about it and we began saving our money for our hotel room and gas. It wasn't long before we packed our ice chest with sandwiches and drinks and away we went. We thought we were really something going down the Interstate singing praise and worship songs and praying in the Holy Ghost. All of a sudden, the Lord began to speak to me about Daytona. I got this really weird feeling that I was going to have to go back there. As the Lord began to speak to me, I shared with my ladies what the Lord was saying to me, but I also assured them that I had no desire whatsoever to ever step foot back in that city. My life had almost been snuffed out multiple times in that city. It was the pit of Hell on this earth for me. That couldn't be God.

We arrived in Lakeland, and we checked in to the cheapest hotel I could find. We ate our tuna fish sandwiches and headed to the conference. I had never been to a conference, nor had I ever seen a church this big. We were so excited that we had butterflies. We looked like giddy little girls and we had our matching ministry shirts on. We got there very early so we could get the best seats we possibly could. We were so happy we were in the fifth row from the stage. It was so exciting; there was a giant stage and all kinds of lights and it was like being at a concert. We had never seen anything like this before.

It was hard to believe my eyes. I felt as if I were dreaming as I saw Bishop Jakes sitting in a chair beside Pastor Paula on the stage. During praise and worship, we sang and shouted, and jumped and praised. You better believe I had plenty of reasons to get my dance on. I had never experienced anything like it. All I could think of was the days I spent in prison, reading all of the books that both of their ministries had blessed me with during that time. I loved them so much. I asked my Dad to order me some more books during my time of incarceration. I think I read everything Paula and Bishop Jakes had written. One that really stands out in my mind was *Birthing Your Dreams,* which was written by both of them. It was a workbook that I used for my vision from God. It was a step by step prayer and study journal for birthing your dreams, and here I sat living out everything that I had written. The Lord had made a way not only for me to come, but to have the opportunity to bring my ladies to see them, and to witness my dream come true.

It was one of the most amazing nights of my life. When Paula and Bishop took the stage, I was still having trouble believing that I was actually there. Bishop preached an amazing message and we all ended up at the altar for prayer. I remember writing a check that night for every penny that I had in the bank. I said, "God I know you have brought me here for a time such as this and I will be obedient and give it all back," and I did just that.

As the service was over, one of the girls sitting in the row behind me told me that the Lord had put it on her heart to invite me to her church's women's conference. She handed me a card with the information on it and we headed to the car. We were soaking wet and as high as we could be on Jesus. I felt as if my feet were not even touching the ground. I got to the car and put my glasses on to drive and looked at that card and it was for Calvary Christian Center. It was from Pastor Dawn Raley, the very lady that had prayed and encouraged me the day I cried out at that altar when I was in my mess. I was so overwhelmed; I knew I had heard the Lord tell me I was going back to Daytona Beach, and here was the very first door. We headed home and I was in awe of everything that the Lord had done. I told everyone about getting to hear Bishop Jakes preach.

As time went on, I continued to hear the Lord unction me to get in touch with Pastor Dawn. I didn't do it for a while, out of total fear. Then one day as I was driving home from work, the Lord wouldn't leave me alone about it. So I sent her a message on Facebook and told her of the amazing things that God had done in my life. I shared how He had brought me from a prostitute to a pastor and how she had prayed for me. Later I found out that she read my text in her prayer group. Russ, one of my close friends in Daytona Beach who had shared in and also kept me alive in my addiction, had also given his life to Jesus. He had been radically set free and delivered from his addiction, and happened to be in the prayer group to hear my text. It wasn't long before he called me and we both rejoiced that we had been saved and set free. All either one of us could say was "WOW!" It was so awesome to see how the Lord had worked in both of our lives. Not long after that one of the ladies was going to take a test for her food handling certificate. Wouldn't you know it, the test was being offered in Daytona Beach, and I would have to drive her there. We saved our money, packed our bags the day before the test, and off we went. While she was taking the test, I rode around Daytona Beach in my car speaking in tongues. I was absolutely sick to my stomach from all of the familiar spirits that were attacking me. I knew I had a choice of how I would handle this trip - pitiful or powerful. I chose to be grateful and honor God for what He had done in my life and how He had radically restored me.

While in Daytona, we stopped at the drugstore to pick up a few snacks. As I was standing in the checkout line, I saw one of the women that I had been on the streets with for years. I knew it was a divine appointment. I waited in my car until she came out of the store and then I approached her and said hello. She didn't recognize me at first and then as I explained who I was, we hugged and cried. I had the opportunity to tell her what Jesus had done in my life and then she allowed me to pray with her. I will never forget that day. She walked off singing *Amazing Grace*. I was so excited, my assignment was unfolding right before my eyes. He had brought me back to my rebellious nation to teach and preach His Word.

A few months later, Pastor Dawn Raley reached out to me and asked me and our ministry to come to their 2012 Flourish Women's Conference. She provided scholarships for all of us to come and asked me to join her on the platform to speak with her about *All for Heaven*. She put us up in a very nice hotel across the street from the church. We thought we were really something, sitting like V.I.P.s on the second row. Most of us had never even been in a church that big. It was an amazing time that my ladies and I will never forget.

The next year, I was asked to come back and speak with Pastor Jim Raley at the Total Church Conference. I had the privilege of speaking with him on a sermon called *After This*. I talked about what happened after 26 years of addiction and was able to glorify God through my testimony. The following night, I sat on the second row of the church eagerly awaiting Bishop Jakes' preaching. A man sitting next to me introduced himself and told me how much he enjoyed hearing my testimony. When he told me his name, I realized I was sitting next to the very judge who had sent me to prison. At that time, I had the opportunity to thank him and tell him that going to prison was the very best thing that happened to me. Because of his mercy, I was spared fifteen years in prison because he had sentenced me to a year and a day with six months drug treatment. When I was in prison, I had made a list of people who I wanted to thank and once again God brought me full circle and allowed me to have the opportunity to be a witness for Him and to be able to thank this judge who had helped save my life.

CHAPTER 15
FULL CIRCLE

I continued in Bible School and on December 13, 2013, exactly eight years from the day I gave my life to Christ, I walked across the platform to receive my doctorate. Standing there in my graduation robe, I knew absolutely nothing was impossible with God. Here I was the little girl who never did well in school standing with my degree in my hand.

From my prior visits to Daytona Beach, I began to feel the pull and see the need for a discipleship program in that area. I felt God was calling me back to Daytona for more than a visit. My flesh struggled with the idea. First of all, I didn't know how it would happen financially. Second, it had been the pits of Hell on earth for me. I prayed and fasted and cried out to God for direction. As I was working in my salon one day, I received a phone call from and eighty three year old lady who wanted to have coffee. She had heard me speak and share my testimony and wanted to sow into our ministry. It was at that time she wrote a $10,000 check for the ministry. That was my confirmation. I knew I had to move to back to the Daytona Beach area.

I met a couple who had a foster care ministry and a living compound. There was a 2 -1/2 bedroom, 2 bathroom apartment upstairs and a separate 2 bedroom apartment downstairs. They graciously rented the upstairs apartment to me so we could start a Radical Restoration Discipleship program. My vision was to have discipleship homes in other areas so that no man or woman would have to leave prison without the support and transformation they need to make it; and the vision had just expanded. I knew I would have to move there to birth this program. My flesh screamed, but my spirit was at peace.

Through the first year and half, twelve ladies and I stayed in the upstairs apartment. Needless to say, we were bursting at the seams for a year until we were able to occupy the two bedroom apartment downstairs. The following year we started a data entry business so the ladies could have jobs, begin to make restitution, and also have money to get back on their feet. Along the way, the Lord has shown me the importance of starting businesses to go with our ministry. It helped support the ministry, but more importantly, I was able to train my convicted felon disciples about responsibility. We had started a dog grooming business and a thrift store in Tallahassee, and now we had a data entry program.

After I overcame the initial trauma and drama of moving back to Daytona Beach, I decided I would use what had happened in my past for God's glory. I went and applied for a badge to go into the Volusia County Jail. As I went to my orientation class, I saw all of the volunteers that had ministered to me through the years of my incarceration - another full circle. It was an amazing opportunity to be able to thank them for sharing the love of Jesus and pouring into my life.

At that time, I met the chaplain of the jail and she asked me to come to a mentorship meeting and to share my testimony. As I was sharing, there were many tears. I passed the pictures of the old me around the table. And to my surprise, one of the ladies burst into tears and said she could not believe her eyes. It was Officer White, the very lady I had rolled in the floor with, fighting and biting as she tried to tie me into the restraining chair over and over again. I couldn't believe it – another full circle.

One day my landlord gave me a call and invited me to set up a table for our ministry at the FIERCE Kingdom Women's Conference. I loaded up all my girls and went to the service. As the host came up to the front of the sanctuary, she felt very familiar to me, but I couldn't quite place her. As she began to talk I recognized her voice. She was the crazy lady with the bullhorn who would chase me off the corner. I asked God what it was all about; I knew I had to be some kind of set up. He told me to tell her what He had done in my life. I said if I happen to run into her I will tell her what You have done.

I went home that evening and the Lord dealt with my heart most of the night about talking to her and sharing my testimony. The next morning when we arrived at the conference I went to my table and there she stood. She began to ask me about our ministry. She had read the brochure and wanted to know more. I asked her if she recognized me and she said "No." So I pulled out a copy of my last arrest picture. There was the light of recognition in her eyes. I said, "My name is Dawn. I used to stand on the corner prostituting and you are the lady with bullhorn, aren't you?" She got really excited as we talked and told me that I had to share my testimony. I realized then that she was another person who had prayed for me. Their ministry would anoint the street corners and would intercede over the area where I lived. God had required her to move to that corner and refurbish the beautiful house I would look at that seemed liked royalty to me. The next thing I knew she had me up in front of everyone. I was presented a staff with FIERCE stamped in hammered metal on it. I knew it was a staff of a warrior. I received a prophetic word about going to the nations and that I would be connected to Washington D.C. We shared our testimony and the Spirit of God showed up - another full circle.

I now go to church across the street from that house. Every Sunday I do a U-turn on that very corner to pull into the church parking lot with my van full of women who God has used me to pull out of that very same lifestyle. The crazy lady on the corner and I now minister on death row together twice a month. Their church helps minister to my girls and she has become one of my spiritual mothers. Pastor Kathy has begun to train me in a ministry process called Restoring the Foundations. It's been a great tool for our program and has brought healing and restoration even to the women we minister to on death row, which now through Jesus has become "Life Row."

One Easter Sunday, a man came off the street while my girls were praise dancing in an outdoor presentation at the church. He told me that he felt he was full of broken glass and Brillo. I was able to share with him the testimony of how God had literally taken me off that very corner and set me free from that same place of hopelessness. He came inside and gave his life to Jesus. We prayed for deliverance and we all went to the beach for a baptismal service. I baptized him in the ocean on Resurrection Day. It was another full circle for me.

The first Christmas after Pastor Kathy and I had reconnected, my girls and I were invited to their family Christmas Eve dinner. As I walked in the house and saw the Christmas tree and lights, the fire burning in the fireplace, and a table set for a banquet, I began to cry thinking about how many times I had been on the outside wondering what it would be like to be on the inside. I felt the love of Jesus and such a sense of home. The girls were blessed by having some great home cooking and had stockings hanging from the fireplace. For some of my girls it was their first Christmas ever. Some of them had never had a Christmas dinner before unless it was served in prison. It was a night that we will never forget. The full circles just kept coming.

CHAPTER 16
THE MOST IMPORTANT OF ALL

The most important full circle of all was the healing and restoration with my three beautiful children. Because of my addiction, all through their little lives, I was a very angry and impatient person. I had a lot of hurts and resentment that I had suppressed deep down inside. Hurting people hurt people. I didn't really know how to show them the affection and true love that they really needed. I was very selfish and self-centered. I was not even able to love myself and I didn't know what it meant to love with a real love.

My children were hurt for many years because of the neglect produced by my addiction and lifestyle. I would shut myself up in my bedroom for hours and get high while they would knock on my bedroom door and beg for my attention. Each time I would get sober sitting in a prison cell, I would be tormented by the pictures in my mind of me sitting on one side of that door with a needle in my arm, while my children would cry and beg for me to come out to be with them. Those pictures of their little faces crying from broken promises that I had made and continuous disappointment that I caused in their lives would tear at my heart. The shame would be unbearable.

As God began to heal and restore me, I cried out to Him and asked Him to forgive me. I prayed that He would touch the hearts of my children to forgive me, too. It was hard to even imagine that it could be possible but I knew that Matthew 6:33 says, "But seek first the Kingdom of God and His righteousness, and all these things shall be added to you." One thing I learned early was to always tie my faith to His Word. I always want a scripture to stand on because the Bible says that His Word doesn't return void. I stood on that scripture, trusting and believing that one day I would have a relationship with my children again, and I am so excited to get tell you today that I DO! God has restored my relationship with all three of my children, and not only that, but I have had the honor of being with my children when all three of my beautiful grandchildren were born.

I totally missed it as a mother and failed at everything but giving birth. I thank God today for my family, for their Grandparents that stepped up and raised my kids when I was too strung out on drugs to do it myself. I love them and appreciate all that they did in raising my children. They did an incredible job. And now, my kids are absolutely great parents to their own children.

Now, I am determined to be a great Mimi (grandmother) while being a good mother to my children. I can't make up for what I did through natural efforts but I can let God redeem it all. As I continue to love God with all my heart and keep him first, my relationship with my family will thrive. He is a family God and loves my family even more than I do.

I will never forget the day that I lead my Mom and stepfather to Jesus. I was at my house on the morning of March 11th blow drying my hair and getting ready for work when I heard the Lord tell me to go by my mother's house before I went to work. I called Mom and asked her if she would like one of my girls to help her pull weeds in her rose garden, and she did. So we packed up and headed to her house. When we arrived, Mom began telling me that just the day before she had been outside watering her roses and lost her breath. She had struggled with COPD for approximately twenty-five years. She began to tell me the story with tears in her eyes of how she was stuck outside and didn't know what to do. She didn't have enough breath to yell for my stepfather's attention. So the Lord gave me unction to ask her if she had taken her last breath outside, where would she have spent eternity. She looked at me with tears in her eyes and I asked her, "Mom are you ready to pray and ask Jesus into your heart?" She said, "Yes." As Lana and I began to pray for my Mom and lead her to Jesus my stepfather came in the kitchen and said, "I want to pray, too." I will never forget that day. It was another prayer answered and the confidence of knowing that one day I will spend eternity in heaven with my Mom overwhelmed my heart. God is so faithful.

This past October I went to visit my Mom after preaching at a women's conference near her home in Tallahassee. After spending some time with her, I realized that something wasn't quite right. I took her to the doctor and on the way home I realized that things were continuing to get worse with her breathing. By the time we got home, I noticed that she had become incoherent and I had to call 911. The ambulance came and took her to the hospital where she was admitted to the intensive care unit. She was talking out of her head and her CO_2 levels were abnormal. They put her on a respirator, hooked her up to IV's and all kinds of machines. The doctor called me into the hallway of the hospital and told me that her lungs were filled with pneumonia and there was a very slim chance that my mother would live.

Because of the fact that I don't like to travel alone, I had brought one of my girls, Belinda, to be my armor bearer at the conference. Upon hearing this news about my mother she began speaking faith scripture in and through this situation. She and I began fasting and praying and calling on Jesus to heal my Mom and He did. This just goes to show that, Jehovah Rapha, our Healer, is still in control. After the report from the doctors, we knew that faith had to take action so we had my mother's house painted. We had new floors put in, and I redecorated my Mom's home so that when she came home she would be encouraged with a new home and a fresh start.

In the past two years, God has healed my Father from cancer and healed my mother from pneumonia.

He is so faithful and I am so grateful for the beautiful relationship that I have today with my family. I look forward to going home and spending time with my Father and Stepmother, my sister and her five children, as well as my Mother and Stepfather, my children and grandchildren. It is so amazing to hear them say I am so proud of you and what God has done in your life. This is one of the Bible passages I have stood on for the redemption of my family relationships and for the ministry:

Isaiah 43 1-21

"But now, thus says the Lord, who created you, O Jacob,
And He who formed you, O Israel:
"Fear not, for I have redeemed you;
I have called you by your name; You are Mine.
When you pass through the waters, I will be with you;
And through the rivers, they shall not overflow you.
When you walk through the fire, you shall not be burned,
Nor shall the flame scorch you.
For I am the Lord your God, The Holy One of Israel, your Savior;
I gave Egypt for your ransom, Ethiopia and Seba in your place.
Since you were precious in My sight, You have been honored, And I
have loved you;
Therefore I will give men for you, and people for your life.
Fear not, for I am with you;
I will bring your descendants from the east, and gather you from the
west;
I will say to the north, 'Give them up!'
And to the south, 'Do not keep them back!'
Bring My sons from afar, and My daughters from the ends of the
earth--
Everyone who is called by My name,
Whom I have created for My glory;
I have formed him, yes, I have made him."
Bring out the blind people who have eyes, and the deaf who have
ears.
Let all the nations be gathered together, and let the people be
assembled.
Who among them can declare this, and show us former things?
Let them bring out their witnesses, that they may be justified;
Or let them hear and say, "It is truth."
"You are My witnesses," says the Lord,
"And My servant whom I have chosen,
That you may know and believe Me and understand that I am He.
Before Me there was no God formed, nor shall there be after Me.
I, even I, am the Lord, and besides Me there is no savior.

I have declared and saved, I have proclaimed, and there was no
foreign god among you;
Therefore you are My witnesses," says the Lord, "that I am God.
Indeed before the day was, I am He; And there is no one who can
deliver out of My hand;
I work, and who will reverse it?"
Thus says the Lord, your Redeemer, The Holy One of Israel:
"For your sake I will send to Babylon, and bring them all down as
fugitives--
The Chaldeans, who rejoice in their ships.
I am the Lord, your Holy One, The Creator of Israel, your King."
Thus says the Lord, who makes a way in the sea and a path through
the mighty waters,
Who brings forth the chariot and horse, the army and the power
(They shall lie down together, they shall not rise; They are
extinguished, they are quenched like a wick):
"Do not remember the former things, nor consider the things of old.
Behold, I will do a new thing, now it shall spring forth;
Shall you not know it?
I will even make a road in the wilderness and rivers in the desert.
The beast of the field will honor Me, the jackals and the ostriches,
Because I give waters in the wilderness and rivers in the desert,
To give drink to My people, My chosen.
This people I have formed for Myself: They shall declare My praise."

He has surely done a new thing in my life. His full circle of redemption continues to work in every area of my life and I have chosen to declare His Praise. Thank you Jesus!

DAWN KNIGHTON

CHAPTER 17
GOING HIGHER

Since my release, God has given me a circle of friends who I call the eagles in my life. They help me fly higher and to reach places I never dreamed of. They have taught me that through battles, eagles soar above the storms and actually allow the turbulence to push them higher. I came to the understanding that when a person sets her affections upon God He opens doors and seats her at tables with people she would never have dreamed of knowing. His grace and faithfulness have enabled me to walk in my true identity and have not allowed shame and unworthiness to keep me from the very relationships He wants to establish. No one gets to where they are without help from others. I am so grateful for all the eagles who the Lord has brought into my life and I intend to be an eagle to help catapult as many others as possible. However, just as I have been blessed by numerous eagles in my life, I have had the opposite as well.

Not long after one of the conferences I attended, the Lord introduced me to my friend, Tammie, at the church altar one Sunday. She came over to me and said "the Lord has told me to give this to you" and she handed me a thousand dollar check for the ministry. She had no idea that on that very day I was praying for our roof that was badly in need of repair and leaking into our living room. God is so good, and He and Tammie are both so faithful. She told me that the Lord had spoken to her about supporting our ministry. I began to get to know her better on a visit to the Dream Center in Los Angeles. Tammie has become one of my dearest and best friends. She has taken me to many places and has been a huge blessing in my life. She is an eagle who has helped catapult me to the next level.

Through my relationship with Tammie, I was invited to the Mentorship Moments Conference in Frisco, Texas. Pastor Sheryl Brady hosted the event. It was a major healing opportunity for me personally and for the ministry. The worship and Word that Pastor Brady brought was truly life changing. There was a special dinner during the event, and I was seated by Pastor Sheryl's husband, Bishop Joby Brady. As he asked me questions, I shared about our discipleship program and what the Lord had done in my life. I didn't realize it, but the Executive Director of TORI (Texas Offender Reentry Initiative) was overhearing our conversation. Tina followed me to the restroom and we began to talk. With the assistance of Bishop Jakes and his ministry, Texas has set up an official program to assist released inmates in their transition back to society. She gave me her business card and an invitation to come and speak at a TORI event. Little did I know that more doors were going to be opened as a result of that most special night of my life.

That fall I was invited to speak at the TORI High Tea, an event for the ladies of TORI. As I flew, seated in first class, I looked around and wondered what the people would think if they knew who was sitting next to them. At the event, the Lord had given me a message on being unstoppable. I spoke and God showed up. Women were healed and set free. I printed T-shirts for them so it would be a special day for them to remember. I was treated like royalty as I also attended a conference at the Potter's House. I ended up on the second row of the Potter's House, sitting next to a retired Dallas Cowboy football player, watching as Donnie MacKlerkin and Fred Hammond led worship. Here I was, actually in the sanctuary and not just watching TD Jakes preaching and teaching on television. He was one of those people who had mentored me through his ministry even when I was in prison. I was flying in circles that I never dreamed of and continued to be amazed at what God can do in a person's life.

Pastor Brady has also become not only a mentor, but a spiritual mother in my life. Tammie and I went to their leadership conference for pastors and leaders. We were invited to her home afterwards and I was so scared. I couldn't believe that I was actually sitting in Pastor Brady's home. They had a feast of delicious food, but I hid in the kitchen because I was so nervous and afraid. As I was finishing my 5-layer chocolate cake, Rose, Pastor Bradys assistant, came in and asked me to come in the dining area where all of these Bishops, Pastors, and people of influence were sitting. I was fighting back the tears as I was thinking, "What in the world am I doing sitting here, Lord?" Pastor Brady introduced me to them as her special friend and I had the opportunity of sharing what God had done in my life. I enjoyed the personal time and fellowship so much. It was a day I will never forget.

Not long after that trip, the Director of TORI called me with an invitation to share the platform with Bishop Jakes on DayStar for a TORI fundraiser. It was called *Rewrite the Story.* This was the first time my testimony was shared on a national and international level. We talked on the program, and then as an illustration he had me rip off a paper that said "Addicted" and underneath it read "Disciple Maker." I was bursting with what God was doing. It was such an honor to share the platform with Bishop Jakes. I was able to share about my encounter with God and how I had received a blood transfusion, and now my life was totally transformed.

During that time in Dallas, Pastor Brady continued to pour her wisdom, love and support into me. I actually got to spend a special day with her and her daughters and celebrated her birthday. We went out shopping and to lunch. I had the honor of going over to her house for her party with her family. It was awesome; we played charades and ate lots of cake. It was so amazing to see her at her home, and to witness the love she has for her mother, husband, children, and precious grandchildren. She probably didn't realize just how much that meant to me. She continues to invite me and my girls to conferences when she is speaking in Florida. Pastor Brady has such a huge heart and would invite us to meet with her privately as she loved on the ladies in our ministry. She had sent us books and teachings and the girls would give her copies of the notes that they had taken as they studied. Her passion for the "least of these" is incredible. God has given me a desire to hold Bible College classes on death row (Life Row), and now thanks to Pastor Brady's generosity, three of these ladies are enrolled and earnestly taking classes. Soon, Pastor Brady will come and we will graduate them from their first year.

Things began to snowball and the Director of TORI, Tina, who is now my good friend, called me and asked if they could visit our ministry while they were in Orlando working at the Pastor Leadership Conference, which was hosted by TD Jakes. They invited an individual to join them who is the Director of the Center of Faith Based and Neighborhood Partnerships at the U.S. Department of Justice. He works with the Obama administration on Reentry. The next thing I knew, they all came to visit. The ladies began to share their testimonies and the presence of God filled the room. He said that the visit to our home was truly an experience that he would never forget.

During that visit, Tina invited me to come to the Pastor Leadership Conference. I went to the Reentry Breakout Session and while listening to a panel of speakers, I received a text from Tina asking me if I was willing to share my testimony. As I got up to speak and began to share my testimony, the Spirit of God broke out. They were shouting and praising the Lord for what He had done in my life. It was pandemonium, and afterwards people wanted me to pray for them and take pictures. Everyone wanted information on the ministry. I knew when I left that room, God was opening doors that no man could shut. He was continuing to take me higher and I was scared to death. I was escorted out of the room to the front row of the meeting. Here I sat between a retired judge and a representative from the White House. I thought, "God, you really have a sense of humor." It was a beautiful day and another experience that I will remember forever.

I was truly walking in the supernatural. The favor of God was chasing me down and all the promises He had spoken to my heart when it was only Him and I during the times of my incarceration were now coming true. And I was able to live up to my promise to Him that I would spend the rest of my life sharing how He had set me free to help others. I would walk through any door He opened and would talk to anyone He wanted me to as long as I knew it was Him. I took Him at His Word and He took me at mine. It's been an amazing adventure; I never know what he is going to do next.

CHAPTER 18
LIFE CHANGING ENCOUNTERS WITH GOD

There are so many stories in the Bible that I can relate my life to such as Mark 5:25-34. It's the story of the woman with the issue of blood. She had her problem for twelve years and I had mine for twenty-six years. Just like her I had tried everything and had come to the end of my rope. I knew if I could press in and push through and touch God, I could be healed. The Bible is full of people who had face to face encounters with God but it doesn't have to stop there. He wants to have a face to face encounter with you. He loves YOU!

It doesn't matter what you've done or where you are, there is no issue too big for God and no pain that He can't heal. I have learned that there is nothing too hard for Him. 2 Corinthians 5:17 says that any man who is in Christ is a new creature that the old things are passed away. I went from being a prostitute to a pastor, a killer to a counselor, from a dyslexic drop out to earning a doctorate, and from homeless to providing a home for others. God has enabled me to transition from a life of shame to a life of honor and favor, from a little girl who felt like she had to buy friendship to a laid down lover of Jesus Christ.

Surrender is the answer. When we truly surrender to God there is nothing that He won't do. Our transformation comes from the presence of God. We have 100% success rate in our graduates of the Radical Restoration Discipleship Program. People are amazed and wonder what our secret is, but there is no secret. It's simply Jesus and the Presence of God. It's finding Him in worship, finding Him in the Word, and coming to the understanding that everything we are and everything we have comes from Him. It's making Him Lord and surrendering our mind, will, and emotions to Him. Moses had his tent of meeting and when He would come out the Glory of

God would be on Him. I teach our women to create a tent of meeting with Him because it's out of that place we come out healed, delivered, and transformed.

People also need the power of God to make it. I can't begin to express the importance of spending intimate time with Him and praying in the Spirit. When I was in prison, I would get so frustrated trying to memorize verses. I finally just prayed in the Spirit and they would come to my mind and once they came through the mind of Christ they never left me. 2 Corinthians 10:4-6 was the first verse that came to me as I prayed in the Spirit. Whenever I need direction instead of calling other people, I get on my knees and pray in the Spirit until I get an answer. Now when I pray, if He tells me to call someone for wisdom or help I am quick to obey. In fact, I wrote this book by praying in the spirit and asking God to speak to me. I know the Baptism of the Holy Spirit is the second most important thing after Salvation for discipleship. It is the fire that we carry that burns up the mess in us and helps start fires in others. The women in Radical Restoration Ministries get on fire for God and love to witness, evangelize, and share what the Lord has done in their lives.

I am sustained by my daily encounters with God. Rising up early and seeking the face of God every morning has helped strengthen me. My morning devotions and scripture affirmations help continuously feed me and remind me of who I am in Christ. It is a critical element in our discipleship program and everyone involved is taught to have personal time with Jesus on a daily basis. They are to Study, Observe, Apply and Personalize by journaling what they receive from the Word of God. We call it SOAP and wash with it every day. Many people want to have just one encounter with God and get on with their life but since I found Jesus I've learned that it is continual face to face encounters with Him that have kept me, transformed me, and sustained me.

As long as we have dark places in our life we are sick. It is the hidden secrets, the unforgiveness, and the places where we are bound by shame that need the light of Jesus. It was only when I stopped running from Him and ran to Him with hands lifted high and asked Him to illuminate my soul and show me what need to be healed did my journey of radical restoration begin. The bitterness, resentment, unforgiveness, rejection, abandonment, shame, humiliation, insecurity, hopelessness and addictions were all healed when I finally faced those places with Him. His love began to permeate every part of my being.

It is a continuous process and I have to stay vulnerable to Him and in a place of humility. I always say staying low helps us to glow. He is not looking for people to climb a ladder of success. He is looking for people that will seek Him with reckless abandonment. As we give our all and seek first His Kingdom, He adds everything back to us. It's important to remain teachable and to keep ourselves free from the distractions of the world. If it doesn't look like Jesus, smell like Jesus, talk like Jesus, we leave it alone.

One of things I face on a daily basis is the spirit of religion that has good people bound. There is a form of godliness but it denies the power of God. Many people are involved in works but don't really know God. A lot of people get religion in prison but it doesn't sustain them when they walk out of the gate. I was told in prison that I had "jailhouse religion." But what I experienced was far from that. I found an eternal relationship. It's the relationship that sustains me every day. I have made Jesus Lord of every area of my life, and it's that reverent awe of God and my love for Him that causes me to not want to do anything to displease Him. It's not about rules and regulations – it involves how He feels about me and I feel about Him.

If you have read this book and can identify with any of my testimony, I want you to ask Jesus to come into your heart and to forgive you of your sins. Now is the time to raise your hands and cry out to God to heal every broken place in your life. Ask God to give you everything you need to truly surrender your life to Him. Ask Him to fill you with His Spirit and give you His Power. Give Him everything you are and everything you have, and let go of everything from the past and let Him pour His grace and mercy into every wounded place. Find a Bible and begin to allow the Word of God to wash you and retrain your brain to a new way of thinking. Apply every word and let it replace the negativity and false identity created by the enemy. Receive your true identity as a son or daughter of the Most High God and renew your mind to the promises of God.

Psalm 62:5-6 says, "My soul, wait silently for God alone, For my expectation is from Him. He only is my rock and my salvation; He is my defense; I shall not be moved." I used to put my expectation in people but now my expectation is in Him. I am not here to be a people pleaser; I am here to be a Jesus pleaser. I always compared myself to everyone and came up short, now my measure is the Word of God. I always say I turned my gun into a sword. The Word of God is living and powerful. It is the sword of the spirit. Through the Word, you can continually encounter Jesus. The Bible tells us that He is The Word.

Revelation 12:11 tells us that we overcome by the blood of the Lamb, by the word of our testimony and by not caring about our life unto death. My prayer is that you will continue to seek the face of God and allow Him to do a great work in your life. You are a person of destiny and purpose. Let God sit on your life and unwrap the gifts He has placed in you. It's been a privilege and an honor to have an opportunity to minister to you through my story. I want you to know that I love you and I am praying for you and every single person that reads this book. I pray that one day I will be able to hear the testimony of your life changing encounter with God and together we can change the world, one surrendered life at a time.

CHAPTER 19
CHANGED LIVES

I wanted to end this book with what the Lord has done in the lives of just a few of the ladies who have been a part of the Radical Restoration Discipleship Program. One day I will publish another book of just testimonies but right now I want to give you a taste of how good our God is because He is no respecter of persons. That means He will do it for anyone and everyone who reaches out to Him and learns to spend time in His Presence.

Alexis' Testimony

Being one of four sisters and brothers and a daughter of a pediatric oral surgeon, you would have thought life would have been grand. I lived through the total opposite. From the time I was seven years old one of the most influential and important people in my life told me she hated me, told me I was "nothing." I was a loser, stupid and ugly. I could do nothing right and I was hopeless. Although I tried, nothing seemed to please her, so I became what was spoken over my life.

By the time I was thirteen I knew how to sell drugs and give away my body to anyone who wanted it. I had nothing else to give and felt like I was nothing. So I began to take what I thought I deserved or was entitled to in a violent way. I needed more money to buy more friends so I could be cooler than everyone else and feel important. I learned to rob people to get enough money to do just that. At the age of seventeen, I was shot at seventeen times over someone else's material things. Materialism became my addiction, along with sex, drugs and alcohol. Life had spiraled out of control and by the time I was twenty-six I ended up with a charge of second degree murder and a ten year prison sentence. I lost my family, my children and after that I really did not care who I hurt. Life was over!

Then I had an encounter with God. He touched my life and I was never the same. God took out His toolbox during those ten years of prison and fixed some of those things that were broken inside of me. God changed my heart and my mind in a way I never thought was possible. He prepared me for what was to happen next. I was released from prison and entered the discipleship program, *Radical Restoration*. It wasn't until after I came to Radical Restoration Ministries though that true, deeply rooted inner healing took place! I AM FREE . . . "The Lord is the Spirit and where the Spirit of the Lord is there is LIBERTY."

Pastor Dawn, thank you for loving me like only a mother could. I am so proud of you and I LOVE YOU!!!!!!

Belinda's Testimony

As far back as I can remember my parents were addicted to drugs and alcohol. My sisters and I spent many days without running water or electricity. We would search dumpsters for food and clothing. By the age of eight I had been in and out of mental institutions and tried over and over again to commit suicide. By the age of eleven, I was arrested for breaking and entering for sleeping in an abandoned trailer and I was off to juvenile. I went and then was released to a program for juvenile girls. By the age of twelve, I quit school and started selling my body for drugs. It made no difference what it was - ecstasy, pills or crack — it made no difference. I just needed to self-medicate and take away the pain.

By the age of sixteen, I was a full-fledged junkie in search of whatever I could put in my arm. It wasn't long before I was in prison in Georgia as a youth offender. I was released from there and about a year later I was right back as a youth offender in Florida. In and out, back and forth; that was my life. I was caught up in a life of homosexuality, drugs, and fighting. I thought my life could never change; I was hopeless and uneducated.

While doing my last bid in prison, I had a true encounter with GOD. He changed my life, broke my chains of years of addiction, incest, homosexuality, and suicidal thoughts, and replaced them all with the TRUE LOVE OF JESUS CHRIST. I then went on to pursue my education while being incarcerated and got my high school diploma. Sitting in a church service one day, I listened as Pastor Dawn shared her testimony and I knew I was supposed to be with her when I was released. She had what I needed.

In 2014, I was released from prison and came directly to Radical Restoration Ministries where I began to find healing through living a surrendered life in Jesus Christ. I have learned what it means to be a woman of excellence and to talk in a life pleasing unto the Lord. I am in awe of my Heavenly Father and the love that He has given as He has transformed my life. He has given me a vision to go to Africa to minister to children all over; especially those that don't have food or water and are less fortunate. I know what it's like to go hungry.

Since leaving prison, I have earned my first job which started out as being a maid in a resort. Recently I was promoted to activities director and since then I have received an employee of the month award. On April 12, 2015 my Dad came to church with me and came to the altar and gave his life to Christ. He is clean and sober now after thirty years of bondage to drugs and alcohol. I have a beautiful relationship with him and have had the opportunity to minister to him and help him heal from the pain of his past.

I am so grateful that God has given me Pastor Dawn as a beautiful Mother in Christ to be a living example for me of how to have a real loving relationship with Jesus. All that it takes is one REAL ENCOUNTER WITH GOD TO CHANGE YOUR WORLD. 1 Corinthians 13:4-7

Melanie's Testimony

From what I remember, beginning at the age of four, I was being sold and trafficked without my family knowing. My dad was a drug addict and I don't remember my mom being around much. I remember needles being stuck in my feet and always feeling dizzy. I never felt alive. My life was completely hidden behind closed doors.

My parents divorced and I would go from place to place. My dad was homeless and lived in a car and my Mom lived with my grandma. So I lived in both worlds. Having everything and then having nothing. My mom, brother, and I moved into an apartment and that's when I began to try drugs on my own. I met a boyfriend who I fell in love with but he was a member of the gang, "The Bloods." Living a street life was not for me, but captivity had made me a slave and I felt hopeless.

I tried my first suicide attempt with overdosing on pills leaving me breathless on a hospital bed. I woke up and when I realized I was still living, I began to cut my arms to feel pain to help release the emotional pain that was unbearable.

At fifteen, I moved in with my aunt and uncle. I had nightmares and would wet the bed. I felt like a dirty piece of trash that should always be dirty and covered in death. I was put in different behavioral centers around Florida, re-diagnosed and put on different medications. Eventually my aunt and uncle no longer had custody of me and I was put in foster care because of my mental status. On paper I was considered an orphan. I moved to a shelter where a lady brought me to church. That's where I first met Pastor Dawn. I have been with here for two years and have graduated with my Advanced Associate's Degree in Bible College.

God has pulled me out of the pits of hell and placed me under His Wing where I continue to dwell in His presence. I am now twenty-one years old and going to Daytona State University and continuing Bible College. I can proudly say that I was trapped but now I'm free. I was dead but now I am alive and only God can get the glory out of my life. "Greater is He that is in me than He that is in the world." 1 John 4:4

Christine's Testimony

I am forty-four years old and have been set free from a fifteen year addiction to alcohol and crack through the Power of Jesus. I had a normal childhood and grew up in Western Pennsylvania. It was very isolated and rural. In 2003 I decided to move to St. Petersburg, Florida to find a better job and something different for my life. I got a job at a restaurant and did good for about a year. But through loneliness and poor choices with men, I began using crack and alcohol to make me feel better and to be able to be with the men. By 2005 I was a full blown crack addict and living with a man who also had a crack addiction.

I was sent to prison for the first time in 2005 and was at the Lowell Correctional Institution. I had a thirteen month sentence for possession and prostitution. I got out with nowhere to go but back to the streets. I was living in hotels, letting drug dealers own me and sell me; prostituting all day, every day for my next hit of crack. I was working with everything I had for the enemy. In 2007 I was sent back to prison for twenty-eight months with charges of sales and possession. This time I was sent to Gadsden where I went through RTU (Residential Treatment Unit). It was a prison drug rehab program. I got out, but still had no plan. I had a desire to change but no desire for Jesus, at that time. I wasn't ready to surrender. In 2010, I fell and fell hard, flat on my face. I was hopeless, homeless and with nothing to live for – I couldn't afford a hotel room, clothing or food because I spent every dime I made from prostituting on vodka and crack.

I heard I had a warrant out for my arrest again, so I found a cop and turned myself in – I was tired and ready to surrender. I was sent to Gadsden for eighteen months. This time I went into the faith based dorm and truly surrendered my life to Jesus, was baptized in the Holy Spirit and received my prayer language. On April 18, 2012 I wasn't Stewart – R39796 anymore. I was free, a new creation. I went to Radical Restoration Ministries upon my release and my life is changed forever. In God's Presence is where my change happened and continues to happen. My life is amazing. I work for a mortgage company. I love my job. I am trusted and depended on; people love me now. They don't run away from me and best of all, I love myself. All this is only possible through God's never ending love and sacrifice for me. I have been out of prison for three years now. I work for God. Remember, "Nothing is impossible with God." Luke 1:37

Lauren's Testimony

I grew up in a Christian family. Since the day I was born, I was in church. I attended every service, knew every hymn and could quote scripture before I was old enough to read and write. My upbringing was strict, controlled and disciplined. Although my parents loved me very much, our home and hearts were ruled by religion. Throughout the first eighteen years of my life, I did everything I could to live up to the standard of by what my church and my parents taught me about being a "good" Christian. For years I was plagued by a self-defeating attitude and an unhealthy, imbalanced view of myself and my ability to please God. During my freshman year at college, I was drugged, beaten and raped at a party. That night I lost more than my virginity, I lost my faith in the church, my trust in God and the little bit of self-worth that I had left. After so many years of feeling inadequate in the eyes of the world and in the eyes of God, and too ashamed and scared to confide in my family, I kept quiet about what happened. I allowed seeds of anger, hatred, depression, and loneliness to take root in my heart, and eventually turned to drugs to numb the constant pain and the quiet chaos I was living in every day.

Over the course of ten years, I went from being a "good Christian girl" to an IV drug user living in my car, cooking methamphetamine, and strung out on pain pills. I abandoned my two small children and severed all ties with my family. On October 24, 2013, I was arrested for the first time and charged with possession of meth. I was sentenced to thirteen months DOC. During my time in prison, I reconnected with my children and family. I reached out to God again and began reading my Bible and attending church services. I even became a part of the faith-based dorm program.

I left prison confident that I could live clean and sober and three weeks after my release, I relapsed. On July 6, 2015, I reached out to Pastor Dawn. I had been up for eight days on meth and heroine. I was living in a pay-by-the-week hotel with no job, no money and no hope. I had sold everything I owned, including my body, so my boyfriend and I could get high. I was desperate for a change, desperate for a life and willing to do whatever it took to break the chains that held me in bondage.

Pastor Dawn told me I could come and detox at Radical Restoration Ministries. I hung up the phone, went into my hotel room and stuck a needle in my arm for the very last time. As I packed my bags to leave, my then boyfriend stood over me picking bugs out of my hair that weren't actually there.

Within seconds of meeting Pastor Dawn, I knew I wanted whatever she had and soon realized exactly what I was missing all those years. It was the all-consuming, awe-inspiring, unconditional love of Jesus Christ. She had an intimate relationship with Jesus and all I had ever had was intimidating religion. I now experience and understand the love Jesus and now I have surrendered my life to Christ Jesus, my Lord and Savior. No meeting, no rehab, and no length of incarceration could have changed me – Jesus is my only hope for true freedom for we all fall short of the Glory of God. The Word tells us that whom the son sets free is free indeed, and indeed I have been set FREE! What could one REAL encounter with God do for you?

Susan's Testimony
From Desperately Seeking Susan to Desperately Seeking GOD

I grew up in a good family, a family that loved me. My parents divorced when I was young and I lived with my mother and two sisters. I was the youngest of three. My mother worked a lot to take care of us girls. I grew up very fast. I was self-conscience and never felt like I fit in. At a very young age, I was seeking approval from boys. I lost my virginity at fourteen and by sixteen I had an abortion. I became very rebellious, skipping school, and hanging out with a bad crowd that smoked cigarettes and pot, drank, and huffed gas. You name it; I did it anything to make me feel good because inside I just felt empty.

By the time I was twenty-one, I had two children. I ended up in one abusive relationship after another. I turned to a destructive marriage and an opiate addiction. In 1995, I was pregnant with my third child. I was still using opiates throughout my pregnancy and taking it into my veins. My son was born with lung disease and eighteen days after he was born, I held him in my arms when he died. The guilt and shame were too much. I failed my other two children and now this. The devil had already consumed so much from my life but it gets worse. I began a crack addiction. Doing both crack and injecting opiates, I had a $500 to $1,000 a day habit. I began prostituting to support my habit. I just didn't care, always hoping the next john or next hit would take me out. I ended up in a very physical and mentally abusive relationship and began self-harming. The first time I cut myself was to get him to stop beating on me. I finally found the release I was looking for and I could finally manifest on the outside what I was feeling on the inside.

After many rehabs and mental institutions and being incarcerated four times and still feeling the same way, I met Pastor Dawn at a revival in 2013 at Florida Women's Reception Center. I had heard of her story and then God placed this woman of strong faith in my path. The seed had been planted because her story was so much like my own. I knew if He did that in her life He would do it in mine. Two and a half years later, I was released into her discipleship program. In just a short time, God started doing amazing things in my life. He is breaking down walls and years of hurt, building me up in Him and in faith. It has all become so clear with fasting and prayer that I have salvation, and the Presence of Jesus Christ has overwhelmed me.

Jessica's Testimony

I am twenty-nine years old. At the age of twelve, I began smoking pot to fit in with my older siblings and friends. I had everything a child could ever want growing up from material items to a loving family, yet I still felt incomplete. For the next 17 years, I continued to use drugs. I would try to stay sober and tried many rehabs. None were successful for very long. To everyone around me I had a great life and should have been so happy, yet I felt so miserable inside. I was angry at myself for not being happy. My addiction began to spiral out of control. I was taking deadly amounts of heroin, Xanax, and pain pills daily. I overdosed three times within a month and a half, waking up strapped to a hospital bed or a respirator in intensive care. I was told I shouldn't have survived. I know God had to have a purpose for my life.

Not a week later Pastor Dawn had come to Indiana to open up a Dream Center. The ladies from my church set up a meeting for me to meet with her. Moments after meeting with her, I knew I wanted what she had. She asked me if I wanted to go home with her and I quickly said yes. I flew home to Florida with her the next day. God has done amazing things in my life in just a month. He has set me free from a seventeen year drug addiction. I no longer have to feel angry and hopeless searching for something to fill my empty places. My heart is filled with Jesus and I can't wait to see what He has planned for my life. I thank GOD every day for saving my life!

Hollie's Testimony

In 2008, after twenty-five years of being in some form of addiction, I was a single mother of two, pregnant, homeless, jobless, and still searching. I had been partially raised by my grandparents because my mother was a severe drug addict and unable to be a mother. When I was with my grandparents I was surrounded by love and life was filled with God. I went to church, participated in church activities, church camp, choir, but then would have to go home. I lived between two homes, one filled with light and one with darkness. I always ended up in the darkness. When my mother committed suicide, I was fourteen and my life became completely worthless.

During those twenty-five years, I would search for God but it was something I could never really reach or sustain. In 2008, when I was at yet another bottom, I did the only thing I knew and one Sunday morning, I went to church. I had my third child, got a job, a home, a car; all I thought I needed but yet I was still empty. One morning, as I was crying out to God to save me and thinking I cannot be the only one like this, He told me how much He loved me, that I was not alone and that one day He would use me to help others. I hung on to that with all my life because I had not hit my bottom yet.

In 2009 I was about to lose my job and my apartment. I had wrecked my car and my two older children were not living with me.

Again, I lay on the floor in an almost comatose, overdose state while my two year old lay in the other room. I did the only thing I knew how to do and I cried out to God. I ended up in rehab and my son in foster care. I spent the next year rebuilding my life with God not cleaning up another mess I had made. God revealed to me how important it was to be discipled and that I had to also let Him do His work in me through others.

During that year, I was also completing my case plan to get my son out of foster care. I had met Dawn while in rehab as she was starting Radical Restoration Ministries. After completing six months in rehab, I entered the ministry to fulfill another three month outpatient program to satisfy part of my case plan. Having someone disciple me, especially someone who had a similar past was a huge factor in my success. I learned how to have a relationship with my Savior not religion or a few goose bump Sundays. Six years later, Jesus has given me everything I have ever wanted, needed, searched for, thought I wanted and has completely filled me with the greatest joy. I am now raising my son in a ministry home discipling other women. To God be the glory, He left the ninety-nine to come after one, and He will do the same for you!

Gabriell's Testimony

Coming from a life of brokenness, hurt and abuse, I tried to fill that void with using drugs and becoming bitter. I had no hope; I was lost in a world that I knew nothing about and it kept me bound for twenty years. I ended up in prison leaving four beautiful young children behind. During my time in incarceration, I felt hopeless and discouraged and then the unthinkable happened. I had to endure the fact that my youngest son was involved in a robbery at seventeen years old. Not just a robbery but one that left him paralyzed. He is a quadriplegic who is serving two life sentences. That deepened my pain to a depth that was indescribable.

Then the unimaginable happened, something that I would not wish on my enemy, my oldest son died. I did not want to live after that. I wanted to die and wished it had been me and not him. At that time I cried out to God and questioned Him, "Why?" and "What?"

And that's when I knew I had only two choices, I either was going to die or surrender my life to Him. I chose to live and that's when I heard about a lady named, Pastor Dawn Knighton. She had a home for women called Radical Restoration. I will never forget the day that Pastor Dawn came and opened up her heart and her home to me. What a blessing it was. She poured out all the love and knowledge of Jesus that she had into me and I absorbed it like a sponge. After having to deal with the devastation of almost losing a child to death and then losing him to the prison system and then actually dealing with the death of my son, I stayed on my face before God because I could not handle it in my own strength. But God . . . Through Christ, I gained peace; He has comforted my heart and given me the strength to get through each day. Some days are harder than others but the Lord always sustains me with that extra love because that's just who He is.

Today my children and I are in a healthy, loving relationship that's full of support and encouragement. God has given me exactly what He said He would give. Today I am encouraged to continue on living this second chance of life giving God all the glory and praise because He saw fit to save me, so I will bless Him continuously. I am a graduate of cosmetology school, graduate of Bible Seminary College and a supervisor on my job. Coming to the ministry has totally changed my life. I have a new love for Jesus Christ, a new way of thinking and a loving relationship with my children. I will never go back. Thank you Pastor Dawn.

Patricia's Testimony

I was lost without a cause, or so I thought. But God had a plan for me and my life. I am thirty-one years old and grew up in St. Augustine, Florida. My father started molesting me at age three; fondling me under my nightgown. I can remember his mustache hard and scratchy rubbing my cheek and the smell of liquor on his breath. This went on for the next eight years. I was afraid to tell my

Mom because I didn't want to be the reason for splitting up my family. I had two little sisters and I felt like I had to protect them.

When I was in 5th grade, I wrote a note to a friend of mine about having sex. Her Mom found the letter and called mine. My mother's worst fears came true. She asked me why I had written such a thing. She wanted to know if I was having sex or was a grown-up messing with me. I broke. "I answered her, "Yes Mama; it's Daddy."

She called the police and pressed charges. A year later my father was sentenced to life in prison with no chance of parole. My Mom started going out to the bars and drinking a lot to try to numb her pain.

I helped take care of my little sisters a lot. I was responsible for their dinner, baths, bedtime stories and then getting them ready for school in the mornings. At twelve years old I met my first boyfriend. My mom ran into her childhood sweetheart at the bar one night and within a few months we moved in with him and all his rules. He forbade me to see my boyfriend. Needless to say, full of rebellion, I began to run away from home at age thirteen. I would stay gone a few days before the police or a family member would find me and bring me home. My aunt and uncle even took me into their home and tried to help me and just love me. But my rebellion was full blown. I didn't stay there, either.

I got pregnant with my first baby at age sixteen. I stayed with his father for four years. I thought this was life. To live in a pay by week trailer park, have supper on the stove by seven, and keep the place clean. I didn't know any different. We experimented with drugs. Smoked pot a bunch and then started doing coke on the weekends. That made it okay. We weren't really addicts because we didn't do it every day. Little did I know this was only the beginning of a very serious addiction of anything I could get in a needle. At the age of twenty-one, I had had another son I could not care for so when he was only a few months old my cousin and her husband adopted him. I was barely hanging on to my oldest son; he was back and forth between me and his father, who was an addict, as well.

Then I met the man who is now my husband of ten years. We were sober when we met. I knew his history of drug use but believed he had been changed. I just knew this was it. My life was going to be okay. We even got married to the Rascal Flatt's song, "God Blessed the Broken Road." This new found serenity was short lived.

My son's father got busted for selling OxyContin while my son was in the house. Children and Family Services came to me to administer a drug test. Of course I could not pass it. I had opiates in my system. I thought if I just put it off a few days the pills will be out of my system and I would be able to keep my son. That wasn't the case because a "no show" is equivalent to a positive drug test. Needless to say I lost my son to my mother-in-law. Thank God, he didn't have to go into state foster care. My same aunt and uncle that had tried to help me were willing to take him. Instead of doing the right thing and completing my case plan to get my son back, I used more drugs. I hated myself for losing my son. I felt like the worst mother ever. My drinking Captain Morgan and snorting oxy 80's on the weekends soon turned into 40 cc's of liquid OxyContin in a syringe in my arm. I became pregnant with my third son and couldn't stop using.

My husband had a good paying job. We had a nice home and could have raised a beautiful family in it. We lost it all to the almighty syringe. He ended up using, too. I was arrested for strong armed robbery and lost my third son when he was four months old. I was sentenced to prison for thirteen months. I got out of prison went back home and picked up where I left off. At age twenty-three, I was headed to prison, for another eighteen months of my life. I was released in December 2010. I didn't go back to St. Augustine. I did good for about four years, and even had good jobs. I was still missing something in my life. I still felt empty and lost. In September 2012 I moved back to St. Augustine to be with my husband who had just gotten out of prison. After all we were both sober again. We could really make it now – right? Wrong - within six months we were using again. I had truly hit rock bottom. Spun out of my mind, hearing voices - demons) and weighing 88 pounds, I was without hope. So I thought. I thought wrong. Being up for about nine days, laying on the floor of a room in someone's house trying to find a vein to get my fix, blood running down my arm, is where I met my Savior Jesus Christ. He met me right there on that floor. His Voice silenced the demon voices and He told me that He loved me and to get up off that floor because He has more for me.

I surrendered my life to Jesus that day. An hour later I was arrested again. He had saved my life again. I was sentenced to prison once again. This time was truly different. I wasn't alone anymore. I had my Savior with me. He promised to never leave me nor forsake me. While incarcerated, a girl in the dorm knew I was being released soon and gave me a pamphlet to Radical Restoration Ministries. I knew this was the place for me. I went to the chapel to meet Pastor Dawn. She taught Bible College there every Thursday and Friday. She accepted me into her program. I have been here nine months now, and in this time God has restored not only my oldest son to me but I now have a great relationship with my father. I plan on going to see him as soon as I am able. All I can say is that there is power in the name of Jesus!!! As soon as I called on His Name I was free. His Word says in John 8:36, "Therefore if the Son makes you free, you shall be free indeed."

God is no respecter of persons. What He's done for me and what He has done in the lives of these women, He wants to do for you. There is hope in Jesus Christ. I pray for a new day to dawn in your life.

-   Pastor Dawn

CONTACT INFORMATION

Radical Restoration Ministries and Dr. Dawn Knighton

For more information on Radical Restoration Ministries and Dr. Dawn Knighton, please go to RadicalRestorationMinistries.com. You can also "Like" Radical Restoration Ministries on Facebook.

To contact the ministry for speaking engagements, consulting, training seminars on residential rehabilitation programs or for placement: RadicalRestorationMinistries@gmail.com

To donate please go to our website or mail checks to:

Radical Restoration Ministries
P.O.Box 2845
Ormond Beach, FL, 32175